PRAISE FOR TRIPPING POINTS

"The Business Transition Planning process has transformed my business and improved relationships with my family. I owe its success to my people and advisors.

ED GERBER, FOUNDER AND CEO
THE ENERGETIC COMPANIES

"I have been working with LeadershipOne on a transition plan to build a stronger management team. In the process, they are helping us avoid the Tripping Points. Hal and Kurt's new book puts the spotlight on the critical areas to prepare a company to go to the next level."

KEN GROSSMAN, PRESIDENT/FOUNDER
SIERRA NEVADA BREWING CO., INC.

"Kurt and Hal have really captured the essence of business transition planning. This is a MUST READ for all businesses. They have made a wonderful contribution to addressing the inevitable changes that we all face and can help keep alive and enhance the dreams that were originally created."

ROBERT L. LORBER PH.D
CEO LORBER KAMAI CONSULTING
CO-AUTHOR: *PUTTING THE ONE MINUTE MANAGER TO WORK*

"Transitioning a family business from one generation to the next is high in emotion and risk. Kurt and Hal aptly identify the critical "tripping points" as well as the steps to avoid chaos. This book should be required reading for every family enterprise."

DAVID LUCCHETTI, CEO
PACIFIC COAST BUILDING PRODUCTS

"This book turns the academics of business transition into an understandable and practical tool for every business owner. While the book doesn't make it easier to face some of these inevitable situations, it does help identify that there is or may be an issue and if you don't at least recognize the problem, you can never solve it. A great help for any size business."

KEN MONROE, PRESIDENT
HOLT OF CALIFORNIA–CATERPILLAR

"A must read for any business founder, family member involved in a family business, or a CEO of a privately held business."

MICHAEL J. NEWELL, PRESIDENT
CRYSTAL CREAM & BUTTER CO.

"These guys know their stuff. Our company has learned–and implemented–critical transition knowledge. It works!"

JIM PERRY, PRESIDENT
THE ALLIANCE PORTFOLIO

"I think we have encountered each one of these tripping points. It is only with the discipline of a Business Transition Plan that we have been able to transform our company through the highs and lows of the business cycle. Hal and Kurt have nailed it and have presented the tool on how to manage your business through tough times."

GARY SMITH, OWNER AND PRESIDENT, SOLVERE

"Great book! Tells the story of my life. Brings together many wide ranging concepts to focus on a topic that every business owner eventually needs to consider–how to transition your business."

JIM TILTON, PRESIDENT
TILTON PACIFIC CONSTRUCTION, INC.

TRIPPING POINTS™

SEVEN CRITICAL ISSUES

OF

BUSINESS TRANSITION PLANNING™

Kurt Glassman
&
Hal Johnson

IONIC

PRESS

Davis, CA

Tripping Points: *Seven Critical Issues of Business Transition Planning*™

Published by Ionic Press
P.O. Box 4040
Davis, CA 95617

Library of Congress Control Number: 20063931648

ISBN: 0-9786752-0-7
ISBN13: 978-0-9786752-0-2

Design and layout by Jannetje Anita Thomas, Binding Plus
Images and photos by © Jupiter Images
Author photos by Axiom Photo Design

Second printing: 2010

Printed in the United States of America

DEDICATION

We thank our wonderful clients, who become our good friends as well as the customers we work to please. We are indeed blessed and this book is dedicated to you. Few realize the sacrifice and commitment involved in running a business. You are always "on." Demands and surprises are your constant companions. So many people depend on you for so much. You represent the heart of what makes our country great–that entrepreneurial spirit that keeps forging ahead. Bravo!

A prudent man foresees the difficulties ahead and prepares for them.

(Proverbs 22:3a)

CONTENTS

DEDICATION   VII

CONTENTS   VIII

ACKNOWLEDGEMENTS   XI

PREFACE   XIII

INTRODUCTION   15

CHAPTER 1 – LEADERSHIP   29

    TRANSITION CHRONICLES, SCENE 1   29
    COMMENTARY   34
      • LEADERS RALLY PEOPLE TOWARD A BETTER FUTURE   34
      • LEADERS SHOW US HOW WE CAN CREATE A BETTER TOMORROW   34
      • LEADERS ESTABLISH VALUES   35
      • LEADERSHIP AT ALL LEVELS   36
      • TALENT, KNOWLEDGE AND SKILL   37
      • LEADERS SEE OPPORTUNITY... AND ACT   36

CHAPTER 2 – RELATIONSHIPS   22

    TRANSITION CHRONICLES, SCENE 2   22
    COMMENTARY   48
      • IMPACT ON PERFORMANCE CAPABILITY   48
      • EMOTIONAL INTELLIGENCE   50
      • TEAMWORK – GETTING PEOPLE TO WORK TOGETHER   51
      • RELATIONSHIPS CREATE THE CONDUIT OF BUSINESS PERFORMANCE   53
      • ALIGNING GOALS AND EXPECTATIONS   54

CHAPTER 3 – OWNERSHIP & LEADERSHIP SUCCESSION   59

    TRANSITION CHRONICLES, SCENE 3   59
    COMMENTARY   64
      • OWNERSHIP WILL TRANSFER   64
      • WHAT DO YOU WANT YOUR BUSINESS TO BECOME?   65
      • BUILDING STAKEHOLDER VALUE   66
      • CREATING CHOICES   67
      • GETTING WHAT YOU WANT ... IN TIME TO ENJOY IT   67

CHAPTER 4 – STRATEGIC PLANNING & IMPLEMENTATION   71

    TRANSITION CHRONICLES, SCENE 4   71
    COMMENTARY   76
      • CREATING CLARITY AND FOCUS   76
      • ENABLING HIGH PREDICTABILITY FOR SUCCESS   77

- ADDRESSING THE KEY ISSUES 78
- OPTIMIZING RESOURCES AND OPPORTUNITIES 80
- CREATING A SUCCESSFUL TOMORROW 80

CHAPTER 5 – MANAGEMENT PERFORMANCE – PREDICTABILITY & BALANCE 85

TRANSITION CHRONICLES, SCENE 5 85
COMMENTARY 90
- PREDICTABILITY AND BALANCE 90
  - THE PEOPLE PLAN 93
  - THE SYSTEMS PLAN 93
  - THE CUSTOMER PLAN - MARKETING 94
  - THE FINANCIAL PLAN - BUDGETING 94

CHAPTER 6 – FINANCIAL PERFORMANCE 99

TRANSITION CHRONICLES, SCENE 6 99
COMMENTARY 104
- FINANCIAL MANAGEMENT - BASIC TO SUCCESS 104
- FINANCIAL MANAGEMENT - SLOW TO CHANGE 105
- BEST PRACTICES 106
- WHAT ELSE CAN WE DO? 107
- THE BETTER THE PROCESS, THE BETTER THE RESULTS 107

CHAPTER 7 – PERSONAL FINANCIAL OUTCOME III

TRANSITION CHRONICLES, SCENE 7 III
COMMENTARY 117
- KNOW WHY YOU ARE WORKING 117
- BALANCE RESOURCES BETWEEN BUSINESS AND PERSONAL NEEDS 119
- THERE IS AN END POINT...WHAT IS IT? 120
- MAKING A PLAN THAT WORKS...AND WORK THE PLAN 121
- ACHIEVE PEACE OF MIND AND FREEDOM OF ACTION 125

CHAPTER 8 – A SYSTEM TO EFFECTIVELY MANAGE CHANGE 125

TRANSITION CHRONICLES, SCENE 8 125
COMMENTARY 136
- RESPONDING TO CHANGE 136
- OPPORTUNITY SPOTTING 136
- OPPORTUNITY SEIZING 137
- TRANSITION PLANNING METHODOLOGY 138
- CONCLUSION 140

APPENDIX A – CORPORATE LIFECYCLES 144
APPENDIX B – BUSINESS TRANSITION PLANNING SURVEY 146

ACKNOWLEDGEMENTS

We have the privilege of being the founders of LeadershipOne, Inc., a business transition planning and implementation firm, packed with great and wonderful friends. And they all helped us write this book. Kurt and Hal get their names on the cover, but all our "transition planning" colleagues have made wonderful contributions. As a result, they too may accurately state "we wrote the book on business transition planning." So a hearty thanks to our colleagues: Ron Barley, Jud Boies, Cam Carlson, John Kelly, Michael Kinnen, Lois Lang, Psy.D. and Jim Sabraw.

We had many of our business associates and clients read and comment on the manuscript. Their feed-back was invaluable. So, a sincere thanks to Steve Bender, Rich Callahan, Jan Carter, Kelly Delaney, A.J. Fraties, Art Glassman, Ken Grossman, Brad Johnson, Bob Lorber, Dave Lucchetti, Ken Monroe, Mike Newell, Jim Perry, Roger Peterson, Gary Smith, Harlen Springer, Ed Street, Mark Tappan, Anita Thomas, Jim Tilton and Jeff Wilson.

A very special thanks to our families and friends who have been encouragers and supporters of our work. It's a great ride!

PREFACE

We met in Hawaii eighteen years ago. Kurt was a partner at an international consulting firm and Hal was running his national resort retail company from Honolulu. Kurt was the partner in charge working with Hal's company. We clicked. We found a mutual respect and appreciation in our business values, insights and experiences.

In 1996 we began working together to assist business owners with their adaptation to a hyper-changing environment. This led us to form LeadershipOne, Inc., a business transition planning and implementation firm, with the mission of helping people and organizations transition.

We both have been CEO's, business owners as well as trusted advisors. We bring to the pages of this book insights culled from careers rich in change and transition. We have written this material to highlight some of the opportunities business owners have to maximize the value of their business. We trust you will benefit from these observations.

Kurt & Hal
Sacramento, CA
August, 2006

CHANGE IS THE ONE CONSTANT IN HUMAN AFFAIRS

INTRODUCTION

To the question: "Can you, or anyone, predict changes?" he replied: Change is the one constant in human affairs. Change is unpredictable, unwanted, unplanned for, evolutionary, revolutionary, resisted, welcomed—and absolutely inevitable."

- Stephen Coonts, "Saucer"

"Business is going to change more in the next ten years than it has in the last fifty"

"We always overestimate the change that will occur in the next two years and underestimate the change that will occur in the next ten. Don't let yourself be lulled into inaction."

- Bill Gates, Chairman, Microsoft Corp.

From the world of science fiction to the "real world" of business, change is constant. In our twenty plus years of working with business owners, we have observed a recurring, major stumbling block—the organization is not prepared to address the changing environment in which it exists.

IS YOUR BUSINESS DESTINED TO DIE?

Statistics indicate that more than 70% of all businesses will not survive to the second generation. Less than 10% will make it to the third generation. These facts are illuminated when one discovers that more than 79% of business owners desire to perpetuate their companies and 70% of the key managers and or children working in the business desire to retain control. If the desire is so great, why is the mortality rate so high?

Through our experiences in leading and running businesses, and then later our work with post World War II start-up companies, we discovered several critical issues—or "tripping points"—that keep business owners from successfully achieving their preferred results. These are not theoretical musings, but observations from the front lines, drawn from the day-to-day experiences of entrepreneurs battling to make sure their businesses don't just *survive,* but *thrive.*

You cannot effectively address transition in a business without considering the impact on the stakeholders. We find effective change happens when all the stakeholders are considered, which includes owners, management, employees, vendors and customers. They all have a stake in the success of the business and each plays a significant role. Accordingly, all are important allies in the change process.

Businesses, like individuals, do change–and frequently they outgrow the leaders running them. And experience provides some good news. *Transition planning is not rocket science.* It is simply the result of a clear understanding of the stakeholders' goals, preferred results and a Business Transition Plan to avoid the "tripping points". To do so requires sound planning, a Business Transition Plan to guide toward preferred results, and disciplined execution focused on continually building value.

CURRENT BUSINESS ISSUES

Malcolm Gladwell's best-selling book, *The Tipping Point*, has garnered much positive attention among business leaders. It's a fascinating read about that particular point when a product or trend breaks out and takes off, becoming a significant phenomenon or success. At one of our book discussion groups with CEO's, we observed that leaders might arrive at their "tipping points" with greater momentum and speed if they were able to identify and address the "tripping points" that impede their progress.

In fact, our premise is that you can dramatically increase the likelihood of success, and accelerate the journey to getting there, by addressing the "tripping points." Your business objective is to avoid the business stoppers on your way to your preferred end game.

Not wanting to infringe on Malcolm Gladwell's intellectual property, we contacted him and ran our title of this book by him. Being the delightful guy he is, his response was "I have no problems with tripping points." Thanks Malcolm.

WHAT IS TRANSITION?

We define transition in very broad terms. What we mean by "transition" relates to all the changes that could impact the stakeholders' preferred results. "Transition" covers internal changes, such as to leadership and management, as well as external changes created by market conditions. Transition is reflected in the life cycles of a business (infancy, adolescence, maturity) and, more important, defines the challenges and skills required to successfully shift forward from one phase to the next.

Our firm embraces the organizational change model developed by Ichak Adizez, thoroughly presented in his book, *Corporate Lifecycles*. The model presents a most useful description of the normal phases, or stages, and organization experiences in its development journey. Understanding the phases, and their issues, helps business leaders anticipate what to prepare for in the next stage of their business's development. This model is most valuable in transition planning. For a more in-depth description of this model, please read Appendix A.

WHY BUSINESS TRANSITION PLANNING?

You don't trip when standing still; only when moving forward. But with every forward step, you encounter a potential "tripping point"—a barrier that can negatively affect your business results. If you're moving forward, you *will* trip. You can anticipate the most significant tripping points and, in doing so, transform them from *obstacles* into *opportunities*. We have found a major antidote to address anxiety is clarity which is best accomplished through Business Transition Planning.

TRIPPING POINTS AND THE SEVEN CRITICAL ISSUES

We will address the terrain of "tripping points" in this book. But rather than just identify these, we'll provide antidotes and strategies to help challenge these head-on. Marcel Proust, the renowned French novelist, once said, "The journey of discovery consists not in going to new lands, but in seeing with new eyes."

Our goal is to help you anticipate and recognize these tripping points, and to have a tool chest to not only tackle them, but to leverage them to create value and strengthen your business and its resilience.

Based upon our own business experiences, and after working with hundreds of companies in almost every industry, we have identified a significant number of tripping points. However, here are the most significant which constitute what we identify as the Seven Critical Issues of Business Transition Planning.

TRIPPING POINTS

1. LACK OF LEADERSHIP

2. LACK OF SUPPORTIVE, POSITIVE RELATIONSHIPS

3. LACK OF OWNERSHIP/LEADERSHIP SUCCESSION PLANNING

4. LACK OF A PROCESS TO IMPLEMENT STRATEGIC CHANGES

5. LACK OF SYSTEMATIC MANAGEMENT

6. LACK OF STRATEGIC FINANCIAL MANAGEMENT

7. LACK OF A PERSONAL FINANCIAL PLAN

Some, if not all of these, are likely not a surprise to many managers and leaders of businesses. We have developed and will share in this book several important strategies and tools for tackling each. We will demonstrate how you can anticipate and address potential upsets through Business Transition Planning. But before we get to the solutions, let's introduce each of the Seven Critical Issues of Business Transition Planning in more detail:

1. LACK OF LEADERSHIP

"Man who thinks he is leading but has no one following is only taking a walk" (Chinese proverb). Stated another way, a true leader makes the right things happen. And when that happens followership occurs. We see many business leaders with varying styles and levels of leadership. The leader who consistently is driving for better results and engaging his people in the process develops committed followership as well as exceptional results.

What engages people so that they want to follow their leaders—and make them successful—are those crucial character and visionary factors. Integrity, trust and relationship skills probably top the list for being most critical. Lack of leadership most often shows up because the person in the leadership position is too busy doing business instead of leading it. There's too much working *in* the business instead of working *on* the business.

TOO OFTEN THE LEADER IS TOO BUSY DOING BUSINESS INSTEAD OF LEADING IT.

Some who have the leadership responsibility fall into more of a "presiding" role while the committed leader grabs the reins, sets the pace and direction, fires up the troops and does leadership. You get the point. A true leader makes the right things happen. But even great leaders are challenged by events and changes that affect—or even redefine—what "the right things" need to be.

2. LACK OF POSITIVE, SUPPORTIVE RELATIONSHIPS

Imagine a team of sled dogs and how they must be harnessed and directed to work together and pull in the same direction. Also imagine the dog-team when they are not pulling together, barking and snipping at each other and pulling in different directions. The latter scene figuratively is happening in a lot of organizations.

POSITIVE, SUPPORTIVE WORKING RELATIONSHIPS UNLEASH THE CREATIVE PROCESSES TO ATTAIN EXCELLENCE

Can you imagine the lost potential in not having the people in your business working harmoniously together? It seems like a no-brainer, but we encounter many businesses that are significantly under performing because their personnel are not working effectively together. Positive, supportive working relationships unleash the creative processes to attain excellence—but it won't happen without harnessing intention and focus.

Lack of effective, harmonious relationships rob you of achieving the kind of productivity needed in today's very competitive environment. In contrast to the prevailing opinion that "Happy employees are productive employees," we'd advocate that "Productive employees are happy employees." Are you defining success so that employees can measure themselves and aim at it? Do you have alignment to foster positive *relation-*

ships and *results*? Are your team members pulling in the same direction?

3. LACK OF OWNERSHIP/LEADERSHIP SUCCESSION PLAN

Survival of a business is predicated not just by building profits, but by building people. We regularly encounter business owners who, though successfully running their organizations, are direly unprepared for the company to run in their absence. Their "back-up plan" could well be summarized by simply wishing that they won't ever need one. But quick transitions in ownership/leadership can lead to quick disasters. Effectively transitioning a business requires thoughtful planning and preparation to design and ensure the best results.

THERE IS NO SUCCESS WITHOUT SUCCESSION.

A few big companies, such as General Electric, are excellent at developing leadership and successors at every level. Smaller and mid-size businesses can benefit greatly by emulating how world-class companies design themselves to thrive through succession and other transitions. Getting the best and most desired results in transitioning a business is not usually compatible with a quick process. Possessing an ownership and leadership succession plan is a valuable form of risk management. It is crucial to understand that there is no success without succession. Nowhere is the adage more appropriate: "To fail to plan is to plan to fail."

GOALS WITHOUT OB-JECTIVES AND FOL-LOW-THROUGH ARE NOT GOALS—THEY'RE MERELY WISHFUL THINKING.

4. Lack of a process to implement strategic changes

It's important to remember that yesterday's answer may have nothing to do with today's problem. Many businesses lack a clear, reliable process to implement changes that create improvements in business operations and deliver improved stakeholder value. The strategic planning process in which many businesses engage results in creating goals that look perfect on paper but, when evaluated a year later, were never actually translated into performance. Why? No implementation process was created—and thus little or no execution actually happened.

But what about companies that do develop thorough plans and set goals? Many businesses set goals that are specific enough to be transformed into reality. There's no avoiding the fact that "action" is at the heart of traction. Goals without objectives and follow-through are not goals—they're merely wishful thinking. And because many entrepreneurs lack tools to implement and deploy their strategic goals, we've developed them and explain them in this book.

5. Lack of systematic management

"If you don't like the harvest you're getting, check the seeds you're planting." Companies with sound management achieve what they anticipate. That is what good management practices accomplish: predictability. And two key contributors to that predictability are good

> If you don't like the harvest you're getting, check the seeds you're planting.

systems and training. Systems help create predictable success. Training helps the people use the systems effectively while building their skills.

Yet, it is alarming how few businesses have systems or people development strategies, and follow them. Systems need to be a dynamic, ever improving, and part of the business cycle. Work flow needs to be mapped, identifying the relationships among the key systems, then evaluated and improved. Employee strengths need to be leveraged. That's what successful companies are doing. A strategy requires a system designed to produce its outcome through leveraging both business opportunities and internal resources. Systems require systematic management.

TOO MANY BUSINESSES ARE "TAKING WHAT THEY GET" RATHER THAN DEVELOPING INITIATIVES TO "GET WHAT THEY NEED AND WANT."

6. LACK OF STRATEGIC FINANCIAL MANAGEMENT

Many business leaders don't know what each of their products or services contributes to the bottom line. Where are the profits coming from—and why? And what should we be doing to make it better? Too many businesses are "taking what they get" rather than developing initiatives to "get what they need and want." Strategic financial management identifies first what must be done to achieve the desired results, and then creates the steps to ensuring it happens.

7. LACK OF A PERSONAL FINANCIAL PLAN

We often "get the call" when business owners arrive at a point where they want, need, or have to slow down, but discover they are not financially prepared to slow down or step out of their business. A common pattern we see is the entrepreneur-business owner "is" the busi-

A COMMON PATTERN— THE ENTREPRENEUR-BUSINESS OWNER "IS" THE BUSINESS.

ness. They are trapped because their net worth resides in the business and they are indispensable to the daily operations. Financial decisions they've made while putting out daily fires have perhaps even destroyed future value of their business, rather than enhancing it and creating options for them to exercise.

How can you monetize the value of your business so the business you gave your life to gives back to you when you're ready to move on? A personal financial plan is your personal map to designing a plan to make the business work for you when you're ready to live without it.

WHAT IS BUSINESS TRANSITION PLANNING?

Every leader needs a map to identify the territory they're conquering. But the best map is worthless without a compass.

And that is what this book is about—helping you not only define your map to success, but to navigate the sometimes hostile territory between where you are today and your preferred results.

In the following pages, we introduce you to the Business Transition Planning Process. The "Coke syrup" in the process is: (a) identifying the tripping points, (b) developing and prioritizing the transition plan, (c) making sure all critical issues are addressed, (d) identifying team members and assigning responsibilities and due dates and (e) implementing a management system to ensure accountability and to achieve the preferred results.

If you want to create a comprehensive, and successful, transition plan, here are the Seven Critical Issues you must address:

1. LEADERSHIP

2. RELATIONSHIPS

3. OWNERSHIP AND LEADERSHIP SUCCESSION

4. STRATEGIC PLANNING & IMPLEMENTATION

5. MANAGEMENT PERFORMANCE—PREDICTABILITY & BALANCE

6. FINANCIAL PERFORMANCE

7. PERSONAL FINANCIAL OUTCOME

THE CHRONICLES

The art in the business transition planning process is to be able to identify a tripping point and turn an issue into an *opportunity*.

To help you, we have prepared *The Transition Chronicles*. In the pages that follow, you'll be introduced to George Wilson, a company owner challenged by the same kinds of issues faced by many of our clients and, perhaps, by you. We will address each of the Seven Critical Issues in an unfolding drama that threatens George, his wife, Carol, and the stakeholders of the business and family. In addition, at the end of each *Transition Chronicle*, we will highlight the representative 'tripping points' just observed in the saga. The story is fictional. The issues are real.

"There are risks and costs to action. But they are far less than the long range risks of comfortable inaction."

- John F. Kennedy

LEADERSHIP

"True leadership must be for the benefit of the
followers, not the enrichment of the leaders."

LEADERSHIP

- LEADERS RALLY PEOPLE TOWARD A BETTER FUTURE
- LEADERS ESTABLISH VALUES
- LEADERSHIP AT ALL LEVELS
- TALENT, KNOWLEDGE AND SKILL
- LEADERS SEE OPPORTUNITY...AND ACT

True leadership must be for the benefit of the followers, not the enrichment of the leaders.

– Robert Townsend

THE TRANSITION CHRONICLES, SCENE I

Woodside Building Supply is a 51-year-old distributor of lumber and related building materials. Woodside supplies major home-builders throughout Southern California. George Wilson inherited the business 30 years ago from his father. George and Carol, his wife, both in their 60's, are actively involved in the company's daily operations. The business is their life . . . and their livelihood. The years have been good to them—though in the past few quarters, the lines on their foreheads have gotten deeper.

They met in college, dated two years, engaged for one, and married after graduation. Their son, Steve, came along two years later. Due to birthing complications, there was to be only one child. They came from similar economic backgrounds. Both had middle-class, go-to-church every Sunday, mid-Western parents. In fact they both agreed that their similar backgrounds with strong value-based upbringings had been a major ingredient to their very stable marriage. And they still cared for each other very much.

George, an industry veteran, entered the homebuilding business by working for his father. He'd been hired at Woodside, his father's business, and rose to manage the cabinet division. But only seven years after George joined Woodside, his father suffered a severe heart attack—one from which he did not recover.

The estate worked out an arrangement for George to acquire the business. The bank manager, impressed with young George's determination and drive, was relieved to have a family member assume ownership, as well as to provide some continuity and preserve the banking relationship. When George acquired Woodside, sales were just under $5 million and George didn't know what he couldn't do.

But the under-managed, sleepy little business George acquired was more "rough" than "diamond." Nevertheless, George set himself to making his business shine. He courted and cultivated relationships with several major home builders—and a few years later, when the housing industry experienced a significant upturn, these builders relied on him to supply an increasing portion of their building materials needs. As the industry grew, so did Woodside; last year's revenue topped $70 million and this year it's racing ahead to $85 million. The frenetic growth has exacted a high toll on all aspects of the people side of the business.

George, a bright man, is a river of seemingly unstoppable energy. He's been able to steer Woodside to great growth while always seeming to have a clear grasp on the company. But now, George's tight grip on the business has been choking out its life. He makes all of the decisions. Empowerment to George means that every employee is "empowered" to solve problems by bringing them to him for his pronouncement.

While this scenario is not unusual for a highly motivated entrepreneur, not much room is left for the talented, senior-level managers he's brought in. But in the past six months, executives that have been up-and-coming have shifted to "up-and-out." Two of his key executives that were brought in to help lead change, have resigned after realizing the low probability that they'd be anything more than mere functionaries. George is holding on to the reins–tightly.

George has other problems. Not only is he losing leaders, he's losing the respect of his rank-and-file employees. Whenever he hears a comment that remotely sounds like a criticism of anything connected to the purchasing department (headed by his wife, Carol), he slips into shouting tirades. As a result, employees are not only not bringing problems to him, they're actively ignoring them because George regularly shoots the messenger.

Nowhere is this more evident than with Steve, George's son and a 10-year employee. His numerous run-ins with Dad have produced both fear and an unwillingness to take on any more risks. Now, rather than being a value-creator, he's resigned himself to being an "order taker." Steve is capable of creating and leading innovative changes, but he's reluctant to get involved because he'd rather steer clear of George's rampages. So he hides away in the warehouse, far out of harm's way and regretting the last time he shared an idea for improving the business and customer relationships.

But there is another issue going on behind the scenes that George has been keeping totally under wraps. George and Carol have been ruminating about selling the business. He has not shared this with any of his key people. George thinks no one knows, just the principals of the company that has expressed an interest in a possible purchase, The Dillingham Group. George was not really thinking about selling his business until he got the call from Fred Dillingham, had a couple of meetings and then started thinking about a big payday.

Let's now listen in to a hall-way conversation between Susan Wagner, the Office Manager, and Bill Harriman, CFO.

"How much longer is George going to be able to keep up this pace," Bill wondered aloud to Susan. "He seems to be running out of hours in the day. He's always short tempered lately. His eyes are bloodshot, needs a shave and haircut and he seems to have a continuous haggard, un-kept look about him. That's not George."

Susan groaned, "You're worried about him cutting his hair. I'm fresh out of a meeting where he almost cut off my head, simply for bringing up the subject of hiring someone for the new risk management position. The only thing worse than George making all the decisions we were hired to make, is when he refuses to make the decisions only *he* can make. He is really getting moody."

Bill responded, "That's not all. I'm not even sure what priorities to focus on—or even if the priorities I have on my plate are still the ones to focus on–we haven't had a staff meeting in six weeks.

Susan looked up and down the hallway, took a deep breath, and said, "With all his closed door meetings I'm beginning to wonder what's up. Do you know if anything is going on? Do you think George would be thinking of selling the business and not let us in on it? I've been hearing rumbles down on the shop floor again."

Bill looked over the top of his glasses, "Who knows?"

TRIPPING POINTS OBSERVED IN SCENE 1

1. LOW TRUST RELATIONSHIPS

2. FUTURE UNCLEAR

3. MAKING ALL DECISIONS

4. NOT DEVELOPING PEOPLE

5. OVERLOOKING NEEDS AND OPPORTUNITIES

COMMENTARY

LEADERS RALLY PEOPLE TOWARD A BETTER FUTURE

The foregoing business scenario is typical of many small to medium sized businesses. While the entrepreneur has brought his business to a point, the company has now outgrown him.

Like George, many entrepreneurs at this stage of their business have developed a finely-honed sense of how to keep their business on track and working. But the style of leadership that was effective at an earlier stage has become a significant liability—their leadership skills have not grown with the business. And when businesses change and markets change, there is a single word to describe leaders and companies that fail to respond by growing to meet these changes: extinct.

LEADERS RALLY PEOPLE TOWARD A BETTER FUTURE

LEADERS SHOW US HOW WE CAN CREATE A BETTER TOMORROW.

We believe leadership is the most important issue the enterprise faces.[1] People become anxious about their futures in the absence of solid, reliable information. The unknown creates anxiety. And when blanks are left to be filled, people will very often fill in the blank with something that assumes the worst. The antidote to anxiety is clarity. And clarity is an important ingredient to effective leadership.

Leaders paint a vivid portrait of the destination we are going to and how we'll get there. They show us how

---

[1] It is so important that we named our consulting firm LeadershipOne.

we can create a better tomorrow. Effective leadership identifies and initiates the steps to engage members of the organization in not only supporting this effort but becoming committed contributors as well. People want to be a part of an enterprise that is growing and improving by constantly getting better at what it does.

The values that leaders model create the culture of the organization.

LEADERS ESTABLISH VALUES

The most important qualities that leadership establishes are the values embraced in day-to-day interactions with fellow workers as well as customers. The values that leaders model create the culture of the organization. And that touches *every* aspect of the enterprise. A key component of creating an effective leadership process is to make sure there is absolute clarity in the value base of the organization and that the values are modeled consistently. Your employees are the first to notice if you are walking your talk. And that has a huge impact on their quality of followership.

THE VALUES THAT LEADERS MODEL CREATE THE CULTURE OF THE ORGANIZATION.

The distinction between **managers** who *do things right* and **leaders** who *do the right things* is attributed to authors Peter Drucker and Warren Bennis. A further distinction is that you manage processes and lead people. The successful enterprise has learned to embrace and merge both roles: leader-managers who can identify the right things to do and then do them right. In this process the corporate values show up in terms of how people treat one-another and how integrity and trust are manifested. Leadership is often evaluated in terms of the qualities one can observe. Some of these qualities, such as intelligence, energy and enthusiasm, are easier to identify than others. John Adair, a leadership specialist in the United Kingdom, defines a leader as "the kind of person with the appropriate talent, knowledge and skill to lead a group to achieve its ends willingly."

LEADERSHIP AT ALL LEVELS

Successful businesses don't view themselves just as *profit* engines, but also as *leadership* engines.

Cultivating leadership at all levels is one of the most effective success strategies we know. Supporting and cultivating leaders provides the necessary resources for tomorrow's challenges.

Leaders should serve as models while carrying out the corporate strategy. To develop the broad usage of leadership in an organization, you first must ensure that the culture is modeled first and foremost by the CEO and the management team. Recognizing opportunities and taking positive action is what leaders do. The organizational culture has everything to do with whether this actually happens consistently and successfully. Spotting an opportunity, seizing it, and taking responsibility for creating a preferred result, is most likely to happen when it is encouraged and supported by the culture. The most inhibiting—or supportive—influence (depending on perspective) comes from the top.

WHAT GETS REWARDED GETS DEVELOPED.

What gets rewarded gets developed. If management says they want to see a much broader application of leadership in their organization, but don't "reward" it when it is achieved, they should be prepared to be under-whelmed. Too much control can stifle the kind of initiative that could produce exceptional performance.

But beware: the critical ingredient in the leadership-development process is trust. To increase the use of leadership, leaders and potential leaders have to know that it's okay to take appropriate risks. It has to be okay to fail, but leadership has to ensure that even these experiences become learning experiences—something we call "failing forward."

Developing leadership at every level has much to do with providing freedom and instilling confidence necessary to make and then execute decisions. And execute is the key thing—because a thought without an action is really nothing at all. How do you grow leaders? Disperse decision-making—decisions need to be made at the lowest possible level in the organization, where the best knowledge and judgment can be applied. In this way, you advance both the people and the business.

TALENT, KNOWLEDGE AND SKILL

One of the few things that most leadership "experts" agree on is that leadership has three elements: *talent, knowledge* and *skill*. However, it is vital to realize, though, that talent enhanced by technical knowledge and intuition won't get you as far as talent enhanced by core business knowledge and skills developed in applying that knowledge.

The famous UCLA basketball coach, John Wooden,

credits his significant success in building championship basketball teams to finding the *talent*, then helping to add *knowledge* and developing the *skills*. Talent is essential, but it is magnified by knowledge and skill. This should then equip the leader to "play the game" at a higher level.

But, hold on. Let's take a closer look at what *talent, knowledge,* and *skill* should enable the business leader to accomplish. First is the predictability of a profitable outcome. Peter Drucker further contributes that "only excellence earns a profit." Successful business leaders develop excellence that enables a profitable outcome. Excellence has a huge reliance on the contribution of knowledge and skill.

In fact, most successful leaders are committed learners. They know that to maintain a leadership position in the current knowledge-based business environment, *knowledge* can be *the* strategic advantage. Our current business environment is distinguished by rapidly increasing change. What is the antidote? Knowledge, and the skill in applying that knowledge provides the best offense and defense.

LEADERS SEE OPPORTUNITIES ... AND ACT

We believe execution is the job of business leaders. Producing predictable profitability has many facets, but the "diamond" is execution. Developing a strategic plan by identifying the key steps to achieve the corporate goals is just the first step. Implementing the plan is the challenge. Not many businesses do it well.

In fact, research conducted by the Balanced Scorecard Consortium reports that 90% of businesses execute poorly. Truly, this is the challenge and opportunity for business leadership.

Competent business execution requires a system with discipline and accountability to bring it to life. This is the stuff that makes leadership work. Certainly leaders have to develop followership to be leaders. But the ultimate test is where will the followers follow us to?

> EXECUTION IS THE MAJOR JOB OF BUSINESS LEADERS

Ultimately we all want to be on a winning team. Show us a leader who can articulate a vision, create a drive for excellence, and execute the steps to achievement, and you will have the unique and valuable resource that all stakeholders are looking for–the leader to take you to predictable profitability.

That's the kind of leadership that can get a business through the various transitions to the ultimate preferred result, be it family succession, expansion, contraction, merger, management acquisition, or sale. Competent leadership provides these kinds of options. Leadership knowledge and skills can be learned. Are you in the game?

THE LEADERSHIP CHECK-UP

- Do you inspire all to do their best?

- Do you cultivate relationships of trust and inclusion with your team?

- As a leader, do you create a challenging, satisfying work environment?

- Under your leadership, do you establish and model clear company values?

- Do you communicate where the company is going and muster support?

YOUR TRANSITION JOURNAL

What are some of the leadership issues that come to mind that you could
be addressing?

_____

_____

_____

_____

_____

_____

_____

_____

_____

RELATIONSHIPS DETERMINE THE PERFORMANCE
CAPABILITIES OF YOUR ORGANIZATION.

RELATIONSHIPS

- Impact on performance capability
- Emotional intelligence
- Teamwork — getting people to work together
- Relationships create the conduit of business performance
- Aligning goals and expectations

"Goodwill is the one and only asset that the competition cannot undersell or destroy."

- Marshall Field

THE TRANSITION CHRONICLES, SCENE 2

Robin, Woodside's HR Director, finally emitted the great sigh she'd been holding through the exit interview with the latest departure. This was the third Administrative Assistant for the Executive Group to resign in seven months—stating that she'd joyfully welcome the insecurity of unemployment as opposed to enduring one more day in the war zone of George's office. Of his previous two assistants before the one who resigned today, the longest tenure was 14 weeks. George's life, punctuated by stress and over-commitments due to his unwillingness to share the decision-making load with others, is teetering on the precipice of outright meltdown. Mary, the current Executive Office Admin, had become his latest "whipping person." And Robin pondered to herself the concern that one of his blow-ups would land them in a lawsuit.

George's last explosion launched an unqualified disaster. Grace, the last Executive Office Admin, had forgotten during the chaos of the day to make a dinner reservation for George and Carol. They arrived at the restaurant and found they had no reservation and no available tables. Carol threw a fit: "How could she do that to us!" George went into orbit. His merciless tirade the following morning left Grace crying with deep sobs–everyone within hand grenade distance had heard the outburst. Grace was out of there.

As a result of the mounting tension, people increasingly avoided one another and George in particular—keeping their heads down to avoid being caught in the crossfire. When employees did pause to talk in hushed tones, the conversations invariably focused on the poor atmosphere, George's mounting bad humor, and the question, "What is going on around here?" On edge, they were tired of seeing, hearing, and experiencing this sad routine. Morale, which had plummeted in the past three months, showed no prospect for improvement. It was no wonder that people, if not out in the field, were reluctant to meander from the safety of their offices except to dash out to lunch or leave at the end of the day.

After a weekend punctuated by George's numerous calls, complaints, and accusations, Bill was on edge himself. He identified with the gnawing sense of pain his colleagues had reported, stemming from being pushed beyond all reasonable levels of work. He knew today was the day. It had to be done. He needed to risk having a heart-to-heart discussion with George about the deteriorating morale at Woodside. He felt sick to his stomach as he approached George's dark wood office and was greeted by a scowl and a grunt indicating he could sit down across from George at his pile-obscured desk.

"You know George, our managers are really feeling the strain of a lot of things that have not gone too well these past few months. Do you think it would make sense to get them together and discuss how to effectively address some of our issues?"

George retorted, "The last thing I need right now is another !≠!!◎★!! meeting! No. What everyone needs to do right now is just get their jobs done. They are acting like a bunch of numbskulls!"

Bill tentatively responded, "I wish it were that easy. George, we all are under a lot of pressure to perform. Some of our folks are not clear on our direction right now and what the priorities are. As a matter of fact, it seems that we're going in several directions at the same time. My sense is they need to be brought together to be briefed on what the overall plan is so they can see how they fit in. We need to identify the immediate priorities and bring everyone together onto the same page."

George snorted, "Not the 'Children's Hour' again. I'm paying these people good salaries to get their jobs done. I shouldn't have to nursemaid them through a hand holding exercise. They just need to do their jobs!

And if they haven't heard anything new from me, then they should keep doing the last thing I told them to be doing."

Bill sat up a bit more upright: "I'm not suggesting a hand holding session. More of a 'huddle' to call a new play to get us a few yards down the field. George, we keep running the same old play, but it seems that we are getting nowhere."

"And I have to tell you while we are talking about issues, George, I know something is going on with The Dillingham Group. Furthermore, just asking your CFO to pass on our financials to them with no explanation from you as to the purpose or objective is one of the most troubling experiences I have been through in my career. Surely you can understand that your CFO should be involved in any kind of major financial discussion or transaction, yet you have excluded me. Over the past year I had hoped….."

Bill's statement was interrupted by George's cell phone going off and getting its usual "most important and urgent thing in life" attention from George.

Regardless of what was happening or to whom he was talking, George's cell phone took priority over whatever was going on, much to everyone's consternation. George listened to the caller for a brief period, started writing information down, asked a couple of questions and told the caller he would get right back to him, and closed his cell phone. All that took about four to five minutes, but seemed like 20 minutes to Bill.

George, beet red and looking very flustered, stood up, put several files in his briefcase and said, "Sorry Bill, I have to go deal with a major screw-up over at Watkins Landing. It seems we delivered the wrong materials to their job site and they are hopping mad, threatening legal action if I don't get it squared away by tomorrow. I warned Troy he better stay on top of that job."

"And regarding a staff meeting, if you really think it's a must do, then get everyone together in the conference room next Thursday morning at 9:00 a.m. Make sure everyone is there, okay? I'll be prepared for a good butt-kicking session. I have to tell you I still think everything would work a lot better if everyone just did what they are being paid to do. It's really frustrating. I don't have time to waste. But if you really think this is going to make a difference, I'll go along."

"And regarding the other matter, The Dillingham Group and the financials, just give me some time Bill. I need to think through some issues and I have just been too busy to get my head around all the pieces. I will brief you when I have the time."

Then George virtually jumped through the door-way, on his way to put out another fire. Bill stood there, shook his head, walked back to his office, slumped into his chair and picked up the phone to call his wife. He couldn't remember feeling this low in years.

TRIPPING POINTS OBSERVED IN SCENE 2

1. LACK OF SUPPORT

2. WEAK RELATIONSHIPS

3. NOT WORKING TOGETHER — NO TEAMING

4. POOR COMMUNICATION

5. LACK OF ALIGNMENT

COMMENTARY

IMPACT ON PERFORMANCE CAPABILITY

People aren't merely a component in our complicated business machine–they are the very engine!

When a leader has under-developed relationships with his or her team, the focus gets skewed to desired results, rather than the delivery system–the people. It's vital to balance people and performance — neglecting neither. We must focus on both *relationships* and on *results*.

> PEOPLE AREN'T MERELY A COMPONENT IN OUR COMPLICATED BUSINESS MACHINE — THEY ARE THE VERY ENGINE!

But many leaders, like George, have been thrown off balance by the pressures of the business.

Ever wonder why one of the most difficult tasks of senior management is to achieve consistently high performance from their people? Getting top performance is possible, but it takes a lot more than "common sense" management or simply applying the latest management tools. That is because most of us, although possibly schooled in business concepts, fail to understand the power of *relationships*. People aren't merely a component in our complicated business machine–they are the crucial ingredient! When we fail to understand the power of this engine, no management or leadership method alone can deliver the kind of results we desire.

Relationships create the channel for great business results. Relationships have more potential impact on performance than any other leadership issue. Building effective team skills that unleash performance potential depends on cultivating relationship skills.

In our experience helping privately-held and family-led enterprises, we have observed that approximately 60% of family business breakdowns arise from neglecting or not knowing "How to get along." Bad relationships rank among the greatest threat to business performance as well as longevity. That's why we must address this important issue as a part of a business transition strategy.

"IT IS EASY TO FIND THE STARS; THE DIFFICULTY IS TO GET THEM TO PLAY TOGETHER."

Social skills support the ability to organize groups, negotiate solutions, have empathy and create rapport. People who possess these skills can connect with people quite smoothly, and are astute in reading others' reactions and feelings. They lead, organize, and handle the disputes bound to flare up wherever humans interact. A high level of social competence is necessary to create a level of comfort, support, and enthusiasm. Casey Stengel, the amazing New York Yankees manager, insightfully observed: "It is easy to find the stars; the difficulty is to get them to play together." That is true in business as well.

Creating positive relationship skills is a crucial beginning point in developing leadership at every level. The
process is part culture, part learning, part leadership,
part team development–and it is central to developing
a high performance organization.

Consider world class sports teams and businesses
that are creating world class results. Though excep-
tions exist, in most instances of stellar performance,
you will likely find exceptionally high levels of mutual commitment among team members. It is this very
commitment that management leaders want to create
and hone in order to not only support superior performance but to actually fuel it and, ultimately, replicate
it.

EMOTIONAL INTELLIGENCE

Emotional intelligence is a concept introduced by psy-
chologist Daniel Goleman in his best-selling book of
the same title. Dr. Goleman corroborates what many
of us had a hunch was true, but for
which there had been no scientific
evidence: emotional intelligence,
rather than "high-IQ" intelligence,
makes a significant contribution
to successful business performance. He advocates that
emotional intelligence, integral to relationship skills,
is not fixed at birth. In fact, he contends emotional intelligence can be nurtured and strengthened throughout life—an apt goal for every leader.

THE QUALITY OF RELATIONSHIPS HAS A SIGNIFICANT IMPACT ON BUSINESS PERFORMANCE

The fundamental task of leaders is to prime good feelings in those they lead. A leader creates resonance—a
reservoir of positivism that frees the best in people. It

is great news that relationship skills are now the most sought after leadership skill.

When people feel good, they work at their best. And, when people work at their best, they feel good. That's a major by-product of great leadership. Great leaders work through the emotions. Great leaders' success depends on their use of emotional intelligence. The leader acts as the group's emotional guide.

> THE FUNDAMENTAL TASK OF LEADERS IS TO PRIME GOOD FEELINGS IN THOSE THEY LEAD.

The boss creates conditions that directly impact people's ability to work well together. It's our task as leaders to help our colleagues "feel good" about what they are doing. Then they will commit their highest levels of performance to the work at hand. The quality of relationships has a significant impact on business performance in both the short and long term, making it an essential component of effective business transitions.

TEAMWORK – GETTING PEOPLE TO WORK TOGETHER

Emotional intelligence lies at the heart and soul of superior teamwork and relational effectiveness. It is the source of organizational savvy that enables individuals, working effectively together, to produce exceptional performance.

Teamwork and performance are a function of relational effectiveness. Relationship is the artery that distributes the lifeblood among the vital organs; the individual team members. Poor relationships foster poor team performance. Great relationships support great team performance. Great results are less likely if great relationship skills do not exist.

As knowledge-based work groups and intellectual capital become a more significant part of a business' human resource balance sheet, improving the way people work together will make a critical competitive difference, as well as contribute to on-going success.

Successful team leadership and management, and even team participation, are inherent in relationship skills. Not only are these important business skills, they are life skills. People who have mastered relationship-building skills have created a powerful resource for the future. A significant portion of senior managers' success is based on skills in the following areas:

> **Harmonizing** – All things being equal, group social harmony enables all members to contribute their talents and skills. Harmonizing provides the creative catalyst for participation—the first step toward contribution. This is the single most important element in influencing effective working relationships.
>
> **Creating Rapport** – Rapport, a close cousin to harmonizing, contributes to the harmonizing process. Rapport signals a relationship marked by agreement, alignment or similarity, and begins when people of "like mind" get onto the same "wavelength" and meet people on their own level.
>
> **Being Empathetic** – To develop a positive relationship requires the desire and ability to understand another's viewpoint. Empathy communicates first that you care; second, you are interested; and third, you are open to another opinion rather than being

close-minded. All three ingredients are essential to developing trust and respect.

Encouraging Constructive Dissent – This is "learning to disagree agreeably." Disagreeing in a way that develops rather than debilitates relationships is a crucial team skill. Dissent, very important in hammering out effective problem resolution, must be accomplished in a manner that does not injure constructive processes.

RELATIONSHIPS CREATE THE CONDUIT OF BUSINESS PERFORMANCE

Relationships determine the performance capabilities of your organization. The delicate balance between leading and following, as well as size of the team or work group, influences the required leadership style, and shifts one's role toward being a leader-among-equals. Then, each member willingly provides followership as leadership is needed. The book *Servant Leadership*, by Robert Greenleaf, exquisitely describes this concept.

Servant-leadership occurs when the leader is the first servant. Greenleaf writes that natural feelings make one want to serve; that is, to serve first. Then conscious choice, based on meeting a need, creates a desire to lead. That is precisely the kind of relationship scenario that supports and enhances the company's overall performance capabilities.

Better relationships in an organization result in improved communication and cooperation—both significant factors for improving

RELATIONSHIPS DETERMINE THE PERFORMANCE CAPABILITIES OF YOUR ORGANIZATION.

productivity. The quality of relationships creates the "conduit" through which we conduct our business transactions. And, the better the relationship, the "bigger the conduit." We can get more and better work-output through our production network when our relationships are robust.

The good news is relationship skills can be developed. They have a significant affect on overall performance and productivity, and are among the most beneficial areas for leaders to mine when seeking superior results from their businesses. Significantly, we are already bearing the cost of our human resources. Making them more efficient represents sound strategy.

ALIGNING GOALS AND EXPECTATIONS

One of the greatest contributors to substandard working relationships and performance is misaligned goals and expectations. We find few businesses have identified a process to effectively address this challenge.

Building and maintaining productive, healthy working relationships requires a process that defines and clarifies expectations. We have repeatedly seen dramatic productivity improvement occur simply through defining and aligning expectations. Having a process to clarify expectations at all levels contributes profoundly to alignment and performance.

*You can accomplish anything
in life, provided you do not care
who gets the credit.*

- Harry S. Truman

THE RELATIONSHIP CHECK-UP

- Is management decision making participative?

- Do managers cultivate relationships for teamwork?

- Is communication in the organization timely and effective?

- What are some of your key relationship building initiatives?

- Can your team environment handle conflict constructively?

YOUR TRANSITION JOURNAL

What are some of the relationship issues that come to mind that you could
be addressing?

_____

_____

_____

_____

_____

_____

_____

_____

_____

_____

THE ONLY CERTAINTY IN BUSINESS IS THAT OWNERSHIP,
AT SOME POINT, WILL TRANSFER

OWNERSHIP & LEADERSHIP SUCCESSION

- OWNERSHIP WILL TRANSFER
- WHAT DO YOU WANT YOUR BUSINESS TO BECOME?
- BUILDING STAKEHOLDER VALUE
- CREATING CHOICES
- GETTING WHAT YOU WANT ... IN TIME TO ENJOY IT

"Once you recognize that the purpose of your life is not to serve your business, but that the primary purpose of your business is to serve your life, you can then go to work on your business rather than in it, with a full understanding of why it is absolutely necessary for you to do so."

- Michael Gerber

THE TRANSITION CHRONICLES, SCENE 3

Wednesday afternoon, the day after the 'encounter' with Bill and running out of the office to put out another fire...

It was one of George's typical moves. The Dillingham Group, located in the Midwest, had approached George, keenly interested in possibly purchasing his company. Though George hasn't told any of his staff about it, Bill suspects something is up because George has instructed him to provide copies of Woodside's financials to their financial people. George, almost giddy with excitement, would like nothing better than to sell his company and its problems, take his money, and "live the good life." George has just seated his guests in his office, Fred Dillingham, Chairman and CEO of the Dillingham Group and two of his subordinates. After all the niceties, Fred Dillingham addressed George directly:

"Please accept my gratitude, George, for making the time to meet with me and my associates this afternoon. My colleagues and I appreciate the time you have given us to help us better understand your business. I am informed by my staff that Bill did a good job of providing the information we requested. Based on our meetings with you and our study of the financials Bill provided, I think we have a pretty good grasp of where you are with your business."

George: "Good. I'm pleased we have been able to be responsive. It's been pretty hectic around here."

"Yes, we have noted that in our visits with you. Frankly George, that's indicative of the issues that concern us.

"Issues? I thought you were impressed with our hyper-growth and the potential fit with your business."

"We are impressed with the business fit. And we do appreciate the fact that you are experiencing hyper-growth. We see a great deal of potential here in your business. But there are some related, complicating factors for us right now."

George: "Oh? How's that?"

"First, your company would without question make a nice contribution to our business group. No doubt about it. There is a fit. But, based on our evaluation, I have a very strong suspicion that you have not developed an infrastructure to manage the business that would make the business readily transferable to our ownership group. While I have not had the opportunity to conduct a complete organizational review, all the indicators are there.

"We too have been experiencing exceptional growth. And to be honest, we simply do not have the management resources available to send into Woodside and develop the structure, systems and the people required to take it to the next level.

"From your comments, and all indications, you are maxed-out right now in all three areas–management structure, systems and people. Here's what troubles us. You have outgrown your systems and your people's ability to manage your fast growing business. Further, your structure apparently became insufficient to properly manage your business some time ago. Lastly, we couldn't transition it without you and a stronger management team. And you want out in less than twelve months after the transaction. It just won't work. You have no successor, nor does there seem to be any in your management group. Based on your own description of your management staff, you have no management depth. For all intents and purposes, George, *you* are the business.

"Some of our managers frequent the same suppliers you do and the fellows talk to each other. Your company has a substantial reputation for being a one man show. We were not sure of that until we "kicked the tires." Now we are sure.

"Frankly George, while your business has significant potential, it's in dire need of a vast amount of management attention that we simply don't have available right now. We cannot afford to divert any of our management at the moment. It's just too big of a risk. I'm sorry. I'm really sorry.

"Here's my suggestion. Let's stay in touch, but we would heartily suggest you need to address getting your business structure, people and systems up to scratch. You are extremely vulnerable at the moment. Your business currently is a risk we are not willing to take on."

The meeting came to a very quiet ending. This had caught George completely by surprise. He mumbled a few parting words to the Dillingham folks and went for a walk.

Later that evening, George, feeling pretty low and beaten, stumbled in to his and Carol's favorite restaurant to meet her for dinner. He slumped into the booth and exhaled a long, deep sigh. Perplexed, Carol asked, "How did it go? From the look on your face I would say not well. What happened?"

"Honestly, I'm stunned. I was going to give you a call after the meeting, but I was too bummed-out. I'm still trying to get my head around what they said. I thought we were on a path to sell the business and go sit on the beach for awhile. This is awful."

Carol: "Well, tell me. What did they say?"

"You're not going to believe this. Essentially they said we were not organized well enough to sell the business right now. Can you believe that? I can't. I just can't believe it. I mean, it's absurd! I just don't get it, Carol. We have a management structure. I know our managers don't always do what we expect. But we're getting it done. Sure it takes a lot of pushing and shoving, but we get the results."

Carol: "What are we going to do? I am really worried about you George. These past few months have been terrible for you. I know you can't keep this pace going. And, it certainly isn't very enjoyable for me either. There has to be something we can do. Have you discussed any of this with Bill?"

"No I haven't. Up until now I really saw no need. I wanted to keep this totally under wraps. The last thing I want is for everyone in the company to start looking for another job because they heard we are up for sale. That really would be a disaster. That would take everybody's eye off the ball. No way. This has to be kept totally quiet."

Carol: "I think you should discuss this with Bill. Look at his background and experience. He may be young to us but he still has had some good experience. And, I think he is smart. And for goodness sake, he is our CFO. You don't give him the kind of responsibility I think he can handle, and it could sure take some of the pressure off you. You just don't seem to realize you are on overload. Come on dear, you need to get Bill involved.

"Well, as a matter of fact, Bill did tell me yesterday he was pretty sure he knew what was going on. And, he said he was concerned, or words to that effect, that I had not got him involved."

Carol: "What did you say?"

"Before I had a chance to discuss it with him I had to take a call from Marty Greenwald himself at Greenwald Construction. It seems we delivered the wrong materials—really screwed up their order–on the Watkins Landing project. He was really hot . . . talking litigation. I had to jump in the car and go take care of it."

Carol: "George, I can't believe you are the only person in this company that can respond to a crisis. And why are we having so many. What's wrong?"

"Now you are beginning to sound like Dillingham. I'll have a talk with Bill in the morning.

TRIPPING POINTS OBSERVED IN SCENE 3

1. UNPREPARED FOR OWNERSHIP TRANSFER
2. BUSINESS DIRECTION UNCLEAR
3. STAKEHOLDERS FEEL DISENFRANCHISED
4. FIREFIGHTING IS PREVALENT
5. NO END IN SIGHT——AN ENDLESS GRIND

COMMENTARY

OWNERSHIP *WILL* TRANSFER

To add a little more background to our story, George's business was not put on the market. Being approached by the Dillingham Group was a welcomed development at the moment, the single event that could carry George and Carol to financial independence. Unfortunately, the business, as well as George, had not prepared for this event. The business was not ready–there were too

> YOU EITHER GET WHAT YOU WANT OR TAKE WHAT YOU GET.

many unresolved issues. By failing to plan, George had, by default, planned to fail. He was trapped, with the biggest opportunity for financial independence sliding through his fingers.

The only certainty in business is that ownership, at some point, will transfer. Ownership transfer should be strategically planned and achieved and not allowed to be the result of an involuntary act. *You either get what you want or take what you get. Getting what you want involves identifying your preferred result and executing a plan to get there.* Unfortunately, this is not the norm. But you can choose to do something about that. Read on.

WHAT DO YOU WANT YOUR BUSINESS TO BECOME?

In the landmark book, *The E-Myth,* Michael Gerber observed that many entrepreneurs start business to create a job for themselves. And years later, many still find themselves treating their business as a job. They are still working *in* the business, not *on* the business.

Planning for ownership succession is one of the more important aspects of working *on* the business—where we address how the business will continue to have a life of its own, a true business entity, apart from just being our j-o-b. The opportunity for you, the entrepreneur, is to create an entity that has value with or without your personal involvement. In fact, the less the business is dependent on you, the greater the value of the business.

> PLANNING FOR OWNERSHIP SUCCESSION IS ONE OF THE MORE IMPORTANT ASPECTS OF WORKING ON THE BUSINESS.

Back to the business certainty—ownership will transfer. Either the business owner can decide how this will play out or either his heirs or the I.R.S. will. A planned transition is the preferred outcome. Further, it is more feasible to transition a business than it is a job.

BUILDING STAKEHOLDER VALUE

Stephen Covey captures numerous nuggets of strategic business thinking in *The Seven Habits of Highly Effective People*. Covey urges, when starting a project, to "begin with the end in mind." While this is really applicable in starting a business, most business starters are initially happy just to have a job. Sure, the sooner, the better, but it's better late than never to pick up on Covey's sage advice and consider *your* desired end point. As a business owner, the sooner you look at your opportunity to build an entity with value (rather than a job), the longer your "ramp of opportunity."

Planning for ownership and leadership succession helps us focus on how the business becomes an entity with a life of its own. That introduces the first opportunity: How does the business work without you? Do you have a successor? Is there resident leadership to perpetuate the business? Is your management staff capable of making this business work without you? Are your key business systems documented and creating predictable high quality results? These are the business "value drivers." The more robust they are, the greater the value. To build maximum value, we suggest taking a look at the needs of all the stakeholders: owners, management, employees, vendors, and customers.

To BUILD GREATEST VALUE, SEVERAL OWNERSHIP SUCCESSION OPTIONS ARE REQUIRED.

CREATING CHOICES

For a business owner to have the greatest opportunity to create value, several ownership succession options are required. Ownership succession can take several forms: management buy-out, family transfer, merger, sale or orderly liquidation. Also you need to consider the potential unplanned options: fire sale to pay creditors, an offer to acquire your firm "out of the blue," or the glorious traumas and dramas of probate.

Ownership transfer options should be discussed and reviewed with all of your professional advisors on a regular basis. There you will be able to structure the optimum transaction.

Are you planning to get what you want? It is not just about the money!

GETTING WHAT YOU WANT… IN TIME TO ENJOY IT

We often see the entrepreneur who still *is* the business. He is so integral to the business operation that the business has little chance of operating successfully without him. So, in fact, he *is* the business.

As you can imagine, that condition significantly reduces your options. Whether you want to leave your business, just slow down a little–take some time creating wonderful memories with your grandchildren, or build your legacy another way, you have choices. Furthermore, you will actually increase the value of your business by reducing its reliance on you. And, having more time to enjoy the fruits of your labor is usually a nice benefit in anybody's book.

THE OWNERSHIP & LEADERSHIP SUCCESSION CHECK-UP

- Have you anticipated the need to transfer ownership and/or leadership at some point and developed a plan?

- Should the plan provide an equitable arrangement for all children?

- Does your transition plan take into account the perpetuation of sound management personnel?

- Does a buy/sell agreement exist?

- Will your business be perpetuated without you?

YOUR TRANSITION JOURNAL

What are your ownership and leadership succession options?

_____

_____

_____

_____

_____

_____

_____

_____

_____

_____

_____

THE ROAD TO SUPERIOR BUSINESS PERFORMANCE STARTS
WITH A CONCISE STRATEGIC PLAN

STRATEGIC PLANNING & IMPLEMENTATION

- CREATING CLARITY AND FOCUS
- ENABLING HIGH PREDICTABILITY FOR SUCCESS
- ADDRESSING THE KEY ISSUES
- OPTIMIZING RESOURCES AND OPPORTUNITIES
- CREATING A SUCCESSFUL TOMORROW

"The reason most people never reach their goals is that they don't define them, or ever seriously consider them as believable or achievable. Winners can tell you where they are going, what they plan to do along the way, and who will be sharing the adventure with them."

- Dennis Waitley

THE TRANSITION CHRONICLES, SCENE 4

Early the next morning after a fitful night's sleep, and already nursing his second cup of very strong coffee, George gingerly held the phone before punching in Bill's extension: "Bill, could you come down to my office right away? Thanks."

All the way down the hallway Bill was pondering how he was going to get back to the conversation he was starting with George the afternoon before when George jumped in his fire truck and took off. It was a restless night for Bill as well. He and his wife had talked almost until 1:30 am. Bill was reaching his limit, feeling he may have to start looking for his next opportunity. The situation at Woodside was becoming intolerable.

Bill rapped on George's doorway and entered: "What's up? Ready for our staff meeting?"

George emerged from his chair and, with shoulders slumped, began pacing. "Bill," he sighed, "I want to cancel the staff meeting this morning. Something really important has come up. Please notify everyone. Then, I need to talk with you."

Bill: "You've got to be kidding, George. Are you sure? We have got to begin addressing some significant issues, or we'll be facing a mutiny. Some of our people have been talking about joining the union, George; this is serious. And the managers are really going to be bummed. With all due respect, this meeting is very important. We really need to have a meeting."

George: "I know, I know. But not this morning. I need to talk to you about the Dillingham matter.

"I had a meeting yesterday with the Dillingham Group—they made overtures about buying Woodside. I'm sure you wondered about all the financial reports you were providing these guys. Well, I have been talking to them for almost three months now. We had our "put it all on the table" meeting yesterday. Long story short–it didn't go well. They backed away. I was stunned—

completely unprepared for their assessment about the condition of our business . . . and me."

Bill: "Well George, as I told you yesterday, I knew something was up. Based on the kind of questions that were being asked, I surmised you were considering forming a partnership or joint venture. At times it was a little awkward–I really should have been briefed. I'm surprised to hear you are thinking about selling the company. Then again, maybe I'm not. Also, I am very disappointed you didn't discuss any of this with me, your CFO. I feel kind of . . . .ah . . . . excluded. Sadly, though, that's no surprise to me. I would like to think I could be of some assistance in addressing such a transaction. And, it would certainly impact me at some point. It would be nice to know . . . . "

George: "Hey Bill. It's my company. It was too early to start discussing it with anyone. But, you've made your point. We need to discuss what we're going to do next."

Bill was very quiet, thinking of his next words. He was really bummed. But one of the traits he had developed was to keep his emotions under control and not react at the moment. One of the things he had learned from his mentor back at DuraTech, his last employer, was to manage his emotions to handle the situation; don't let your emotions determine the outcome. Let reason prevail. So he was working hard to do just that.

"Okay George. I will pass the word that the meeting is cancelled. But you and I have to have a discussion about this whole matter–and what my involvement should be."

George: "Just as soon as you have cancelled the staff meeting."

Bill, looking cautiously at George, said: "I will be right back."

Bill walked down the hallway to his office with a fair idea of what had happened in the Dillingham meeting. He pretty well understood the weaknesses of the organization. They were not necessarily in the financials, although the financial performance was certainly impacted. It was no secret that George was the problem. He was still running the business the way he must have run it ten years ago.

The company had simply outgrown its employees and systems. The staff was geared up to operate a company with half their revenue. There was no accounting for all the profits that were falling through the cracks just because of poor management. George was not approachable on making any management changes. George reacted like it was a personal attack when anyone suggested making any changes to any of the company's management practices. As far as George was concerned, everything was working okay—up until the past few months—and particularly yesterday.

After working at Woodside for two years, Bill had learned that, regardless of the stated value of teamwork, George still made most of the meaningful decisions. As a result, the management group was weak at best. George's tight-fisted and dictatorial decision-making was more indicative of a classic early stage entrepreneurial business that, by now, should have transitioned to a high performance management team. The only thing George knew about teamwork could have been Dilbert's definition of teams: "When a group of people jointly decides to rely on one person." Team-work was more an idea than a reality to George. He even had "Team Woodside" buttons made for the last retreat. People left them in their desk drawer after a day or so. It was a joke.

At a strategic planning retreat three months earlier, they'd even developed a vision statement and goals. Or George did. There wasn't a lot of input or discussion. They were distributed the next week and that was the last anyone had heard of them. Three months later, nothing had been heard of about the business plan, goals, or who was doing what—Woodside's future direction remained a mystery to everyone but George. So the strategic planning meeting led to everyone strategically planning to continue waiting to hear from George. George had single-handedly turned a bunch of fire-breathing and excited managers, all whom he hired, into a bunch of order takers. No wonder Dillingham backed off. No wonder the managers are so frustrated.

When Bill slipped back into George's office, he found George absently staring at the top of his desk. To get the conversation going, Bill offered, "Well, how bad was the meeting?"

George drew a long breath with his eyes closed, "Awful. Simply awful. They essentially said we did not have the management in place to handle our business growth. And, they did not have the management available to do it for us if they acquired us. That just does not make sense. Our management gets the job done. Granted, we have our share of issues, but I think everyone is pretty committed. What do you think, Bill?"

TRIPPING POINTS OBSERVED IN SCENE 4

1. LACK OF CLARITY AND FOCUS
2. NO DEVELOPED MANAGEMENT PROCESSES
3. REACTING TO GROWTH RATHER THAN MANAGING IT
4. INEFFICIENCIES AND LACK OF SYSTEMS
5. NO SHARED VISION OR HOPE FOR TOMORROW

COMMENTARY

CREATING CLARITY AND FOCUS

George had committed one of the most common errors of mankind: confusing activity with direction. He was really going nowhere, except to work everyday. Remember the Cheshire Cat in *Alice in Wonderland*? When Alice asked him for directions, he said to her, "Where are you going?" She replied, "I don't really know." To which he responded, "Then any road will take you there." George did not know where his business was going. Like many business owners, he was responding to the issues of the day, and living in hope.

MANY HAVE PLANS; FEW EXECUTE THEM WELL.

Hoping that he could keep things on track. But while George was busy chopping down trees, he lacked the perspective to see that he was working on the wrong forest.

The road to superior business performance starts with a concise strategic plan—one that aligns stakeholders' values and goals. This plan must be executed consistently and systematically. In fact, intensive research out of Harvard University indicates 90% of businesses do not execute their strategies effectively.

Planning begins the journey to accomplishment. It creates focus, and gives you the opportunity to build on your strategic advantages. But a plan needs a target, and that target gets established through vision. A plan with vision inspires. As a sage wrote centuries ago, "Without a vision, the people perish."

Corporate leaders have the responsibility to create and communicate their vision of the future, and where the business is heading. Focusing on vision disciplines us to think strategically. It helps us to start with the end in mind, and to identify what we are going to create. Vision is one of the most sought after leadership characteristics. It provides the all important context for business goals. And that is what leaders do—identify and articulate a vision, as well as aligning organizations to execute the plan.

Vision sees what *must be* tomorrow, beyond what *is* today. However, having vision is not some mystical, mysterious insight. The editors of *Fortune* magazine said,

WITHOUT DISCIPLINE TO IMPLEMENT, A PLAN IS JUST A DREAM!

"The new paragon of an executive is a person who can *envision* a future for the organization and then *inspire* colleagues to join in building that future" (emphasis added). Vision, is not predicting the next decade. It's much more about seeing what the organization must be next month, next quarter, or next year.

ENABLING HIGH PREDICTABILITY FOR SUCCESS

The essence of management is *predictability*. When an

enterprise consistently achieves highly predictable outcomes, it is under successful management. But achievement requires measurement. You must measure to manage. So, in order to craft a measurable implementation process that will accomplish a strategic plan, the first step is to define the work to be accomplished. This definition of work is the *Action Plan;* a valuable tool to prioritize and schedule what is to be implemented.

Systematic progress review of the *Action Plan* is crucial to this process. Without this discipline, a plan is just a dream! To achieve your plan you have to *inspect* what you *expect.* All good management systems have a feedback mechanism to assure that preferred results are being achieved.

Achieving your strategic plan is a dynamic process, that involves adjusting tasks to be accomplished as more information becomes available. These adjustments are merely course corrections that are similar to the aircraft making adjustments to strong winds. You know where you want to go, but you may have to factor in corrective direction based on real-life feedback.

ADDRESSING THE KEY ISSUES

What separates winners from losers in professional sports is execution. It's the same in business. Take a look at how well you are executing your plans. Are you in the "winner's column?" Ultimately we all are judged by the results we post. Well thought-out plans are meaningless without execution that translates our vision into reality.

Simple? Yes. Easy? No way! In fact, it's becoming increasingly difficult. Great business results are based on great execution, just like in sports, which requires orchestrating great talent, knowledge and skills.

Not only is execution critical , what you are working on matters as well. With all the competing demands you face, how can you determine which demands on the business should be tackled next? Here are the steps involved in a robust strategic planning and implementation process:

1. *Identify guiding values and principles, and agree that these values form the basis for all activity.*

2. *Perform a situation analysis to determine strategic issues (also called gap analysis).*

3. *Determine the vision that guides the enterprise.*

4. *Align values and vision to create a mission to maximize performance.*

5. *Establish strategies to support balanced execution of priorities.*

6. *Determine goals that need to be addressed based on issues derived from situations analysis.*

7. *Select the projects that will cause each goal to be realized and agree on responsibility and timing; this creates the Action Plan.*

8. *Do the high impact projects first.*

9. *Develop management systems to monitor implementation progress.*

10. *Evaluate and make adjustments as needed to assure you are making real progress.*

OPTIMIZING RESOURCES AND OPPORTUNITIES

Proficiency at the strategic planning and implementation process can catapult your business ahead of the competition. Take a look at your planning and execution processes. You can either get the results you want or take what you get.

The Strategic Planning Process will enable you to sort through competing demands, analyze benefits from various options, and select tactics that will enable the organization to create preferred results. Planning enables you to better capitalize on resources and opportunities. It's an incredibly valuable tool that Fortune 500 companies have learned to use to stay in the game of business profitably, year after year.

CREATING A SUCCESSFUL TOMORROW

You can either have what is probable, what is possible, or what is preferred. These are the three P's of the Future. Leaders get to create them. We need to know what is possible first, then we can select and execute toward the preferred, rather than just taking what is probable. That is how you can create a successful tomorrow. Chose and execute for the preferred outcomes. But, you have to have a system and know how to use it.

> YOU CAN EITHER HAVE WHAT IS PROBABLE, POSSIBLE, OR PREFERRED.

Probable
Possible
Preferred

"The best way to predict the future is to create it."

- Peter Drucker

THE STRATEGIC PLANNING & IMPLEMENTATION CHECK-UP

- Are your strategies built around a clear proposition for the customer?

- Do you strategically keep growing the core business?

- Do you regularly achieve performance targets?

- Do you know what needs to be done to consistently beat the competition?

- Do you annually prepare a strategic plan and make it happen?

YOUR TRANSITION JOURNAL

What are some of the planning and
execution issues that come to mind
that you could be addressing?

_____

_____

_____

_____

_____

_____

_____

_____

_____

DEVELOPING RELATED KEY PERFORMANCE INDICATORS HELPS
MAINTAIN PERSPECTIVE

MANAGEMENT PERFORMANCE - PREDICTABILITY & BALANCE

- PREDICTABILITY & BALANCE
- THE PEOPLE PLAN
- THE SYSTEMS PLAN
- THE CUSTOMER PLAN—MARKETING
- THE FINANCIAL PLAN—BUDGETING

"Be a yardstick of quality. Some people are not used to an environment where excellence is expected."

- Steve Jobs

THE TRANSITION CHRONICLES, SCENE 5

This was the career position Bill wanted, but he had not anticipated George's quirkiness. Though Bill had conducted extensive due diligence prior to accepting this position, the journey at Woodside had become an extraordinary disappointment to him. And this recent episode about Dillingham, particularly the way George handled it, was more disillusioning.

George was stuck. He still ran his business like it was a mom and pop store. He'd said the right things in attracting Bill to the job; he just had not followed through. Now it seemed that George neither knew how to change nor possessed the inclination to do so.

One of many things Bill had enjoyed at DuraTech was the fact they were very well managed. He had seen what good management and leadership looked like. He had been part of an exciting management development program that had kept DuraTech growing while nicely profitable. People were important and they were being prepared to take the company into the future, something it seemed only the big companies truly understood and saw as important.

DuraTech management stressed that employees had to continually re-invent themselves or face losing their competitive edge. And that philosophy applied to all aspects of the business. If a manager didn't have his head around it and practice it, he was not going to move ahead. So, it worked pretty well—as much so as any company Bill knew about. And he'd naively hoped that he would get to help transition Woodside into that kind of company.

Bill pensively thought, "Could it be that George has finally heard his wake-up call? Let's see what he is ready and willing to do." He rejoined George to learn more about the Dillingham meeting.

Bill: "George, I'm not sure I know what to think yet. Let me ask you a couple of questions to help me get a better handle on what I think is going on. Okay?

George: "Sure. What do you want to know?"

Bill: "From what you have told me, and what I heard a couple of their people discussing, I don't think it's our financial performance that concerns them. Did they mention anything about that?"

George: "No, nothing about the financials that I recall. It was more about our lack of management depth. Get this–they said I was the business! We have over 180 people working here and they say I am the business. Ridiculous!"

Bill: "Did they ask you about how we approach systems improvement or strategic planning?"

George: "Now that you mention it, they did. They asked me how I was preparing the company to sustain its growth and profitability. Maybe I was a little flippant. I compared it to running a hardware store. I told them I follow the philosophy that we have to give the customer what they want and make sure everybody understands that. If they don't, then get their butts out of here. Frankly, I thought they were so impressed with our numbers that all this other organizational stuff was just so much window dressing. Maybe I misread the situation."

Bill: "Anything about our management structure or processes?"

George: "They asked to see the Strategic Plan, which I gave them. They asked me to describe the process —how we developed it and how we implemented it. That was pretty straight forward since we had just gone through the process. I did tell them it was our first cut at it and we were still working on implementation, but that everyone seemed to think it was a good process. And they asked about our management training.

So I told them basically our managers are responsible for on-the-job training. I told them I thought we had a decent group of managers, who were young with not a lot of experience, but generally knew their jobs and were enthusiastic. That's about it."

Bill: "George, please don't take this the wrong way. I think they were looking for a depth and breadth in management that is really preparing the company for the future. What they found was a group of people running as hard as they could to just keep up, and managing from crisis to crisis. George, you and I have discussed this in at least three conversations during the past two months.

"Just last week we had another crisis meeting about our customer retention program, lack of data, and lack of accountability all rolled into one big mess. Sadly, that was just like every other week in recent memory. George, listen to me: we're not proactive, nor are we building a company that shapes the future. Instead, we are being shaped by unexpected events that are hitting us.

"Sure, we have managers that are conscientious. But look at what we're working with. Henry is responsible for all of Marketing and Sales. He's thirty-one years old, has had one other job in his career and doesn't know beans about holding his sales people accountable. And as for marketing knowledge, reading industry magazines has given him the only education he's got.

"And Ken over in IT is in a similar situation. In the past month, he has done nothing but put out fires and spend money like there is no tomorrow. There is no system to our systems expansion. We continue to cobble things together to take care of today's crisis. I don't mean to be overly critical of Ken or Henry, but we have outgrown some of our key managers. They just don't have the horsepower to get us to the next level. They were fine first-line supervisors. But we promoted them into management positions for which they were unqualified, unprepared, and are still untrained.

"As a result, Woodside has outgrown the leadership ability of its management group—the team is 'undersized' for the growth we've experienced and continue to experience. I'm sure that is what the Dillingham people saw. In the absence of a strong management team, *you* have to make all the tough decisions–therefore, *you* are the business. In its current state, without you, it wouldn't work."

George sat quietly, mulling Bill's observations. Sullenly, he commented, "Bill, you are not wrong. I guess I just was not aware of the magnitude of the impact of our fast growth on everybody. It has been tough. I guess I need to take a few steps back and rethink where I am in this whole business game. I think Carol and I need to get away this weekend and try to get some perspective. I have a lot to think about."

TRIPPING POINTS OBSERVED IN SCENE 5

1. Lack of knowledge

2. People poorly prepared

3. Systems undersized or failing

4. Lack of a management team

5. Lack of organization

COMMENTARY

PREDICTABILITY & BALANCE

George, like many business owners, has not kept pace with the demands of growth. His business has outgrown him and his management style. Neither he nor his managers have kept pace with what the business requires to be effectively and efficiently guided.

In your business are the right people in the right positions and are their successors being trained? How effectively are you preparing for the future? How are you developing management knowledge and skills to effectively execute?

Professor Warren Bennis at USC is recognized for first making the distinction between management and leadership. He says management is doing things right and leadership is doing the right things. You certainly need both. Professional leaders need to make sure their organization is doing the right things and doing them well. In a nutshell, that's your job as a leader.

Doing things right puts an emphasis on high quality business systems. In order to achieve predictable results, your systems need to be well designed and administered. It is management's job to make sure the right systems are in place and can efficiently contribute to desired business results. Doing the right things involves creating an environment where business colleagues are contributing their best efforts toward achieving these business results. Leadership is creating the culture that enables colleagues to participate in achieving preferred results.

This process does not happen naturally. People in organizations do not naturally perform at optimal levels. Corporate culture has a tremendous impact on the creativity and commitment of the work force. The great opportunity of the executive leadership is to create a high performance culture. This takes management and leadership. If we call ourselves professional managers, we must utilize all of our leadership skills to be successful managers. We must become proficient at managing ourselves, our business systems, and our personal leadership system.

> PEOPLE IN THE ORGANIZATION DO NOT NATURALLY PERFORM AT OPTIMAL LEVELS.

One of the most effective processes we have seen so far that focuses on both doing the right things and then doing them right is the Balanced Scorecard (introduced by Robert Kaplan and David Norton).

The Balanced Scorecard provides corporate managers the instrumentation they need to navigate to future competitive success. This system enables you and your team to "navigate" your business to the desired results.

The Balanced Scorecard helps us take our vision, strategic plan and action plan, to create a system that provides feedback regarding how effective our various tasks and projects in our action plan really are. The scorecard should tell us if all our efforts toward championship performance are really getting us the results we want without burying us in unnecessary tracking and sorting of extraneous details.

Navigation and performance rely on an effective execution of strategy. Larry Bossidy and Ram Charan, in *Execution: The Discipline of Getting Things Done*, discuss the crucial nature of execution. Organizations don't execute well unless the right people, individually and collectively, focus on the right details at the right time. The Balanced Scorecard is an important tool that focuses us on executing the right details at the right time.

> NAVIGATION AND PERFORMANCE RELY ON EFFECTIVE STRATEGY EXECUTION.

A well-designed scorecard focuses our attention on the blended activities that have the greatest impact on the organization. The Balanced Scorecard, while emphasizing financial performance, also addresses what drives the company's financial results. The scorecard measures organizational performance across four balanced perspectives:

- The Growth/Development of the Human Resources (**PEOPLE PLAN**)

- Internal Systems and Quality (**SYSTEMS PLAN**)

- The Customer (**Marketing plan**)

- Financial (**Financial plan – budget**)

These four perspectives help focus our attention on the activities that have the greatest impact on the company's overall performance and predictable success. Let's now examine each of the four perspectives in terms of their contribution to management performance.

PERSPECTIVE #1: THE PEOPLE PLAN

The people plan involves identifying the infrastructure the organization must build to create long term growth and development — a challenge most businesses neglect. These organizations are not preparing their people to meet the increasing demands of change. Customer and internal processes should identify the factors most critical for current and future success. The business will be unprepared to address those factors unless the learning and growth issues are in balance. The emphasis here needs to be on people, systems, and organizational procedures.

PERSPECTIVE #2: THE SYSTEMS PLAN

Here we identify the critical internal processes and systems that must excel within an organization. The essence of management is predictability, which is determined by the quality of the internal processes. These processes enable the business to:

- Deliver the quality product/service needed to meet the wants of customers, and

- Meet expectations of financial goals

Measures used in this perspective need to address not only existing processes but innovations needed to continue to satisfy the above two business objectives. Managers need to be thinking of improving present conditions while designing the future. Then organizations need to measure progress toward achieving preferred results.

PERSPECTIVE #3: THE CUSTOMER PLAN – MARKETING

The customer is the business. Is our business on the right track? We must obtain feedback that informs us how we are doing with our customers. How effective we are at getting new customers, as well as retaining them once we've landed them? Too often significant resources are devoted to bringing in new customers without looking at the cost/income implications of low customer retention. This has broad operating implications that impact the health of the business in a very significant way. Customer satisfaction is an important area about which we need to know much and respond to smartly.

PERSPECTIVE #4: THE FINANCIAL PLAN – BUDGET

Financial plans and budgets indicate whether a company's strategies, implementation and execution are contributing to bottom-line improvement. These are the most familiar measures, since the success and perpetuation of the business essentially are based on these measures and results. Developing related key performance indicators helps maintain perspective on the balance needed to achieve the organization's financial goals.

"Setting an example is not the main means of influencing another: It is the only means."

- Albert Einstein

THE MANAGEMENT PERFORMANCE & PREDICTABILITY CHECK-UP

- Have you identified your replacement and is he/she in training?

- Are your people effective in meeting their work commitments?

- Do you have effective performance measures?

- Is your management culture results oriented?

- Are your managers effective in performance coaching?

YOUR TRANSITION JOURNAL

What are some of the management
issues that come to mind that you could
be addressing?

_____

_____

_____

_____

_____

_____

_____

_____

_____

_____

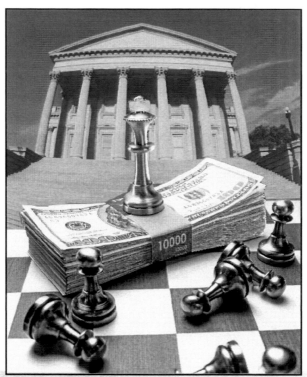

TARGETING AND EXECUTING THE RIGHT OUTCOMES ARE ESSENTIAL
IN REALIZING POSITIVE FINANCIAL RESULTS

FINANCIAL PERFORMANCE

- FINANCIAL MANAGEMENT — BASIC TO SUCCESS
- FINANCIAL MANAGEMENT — SLOW TO CHANGE
- BEST PRACTICES
- WHAT ELSE CAN WE DO?
- THE BETTER THE PROCESS, THE BETTER THE RESULTS

"A man's judgment is no better than his information."

– Chinese Proverb

THE TRANSITION CHRONICLES, SCENE 6

Back in his office, Bill stared out the windows while collecting his thoughts. George's plight wasn't something he hadn't seen before; he recalled a similar situation with one of his accounting firm's clients early in his public accounting days. The client created a successful small business, but kept running it like a small business. He didn't have a ghost of an idea of how bad things were until it was too late. He had called the accounting firm Bill was working for at the time, hoping to find some quick answers that would extract him from a major cash mess. But it was too late; the business virtually imploded. They were making profits—on paper. But, their cash situation became so serious, they were forced into Chapter 11. The business finally was sold at a fire sale. What a tragedy. It was a great business, but there was a serious lack of know-how on how to properly manage it.

GEORGE RAN HIS BUSINESS AS IF HE EXPECTED TO LIVE FOREVER.

Bill feared this scenario would be repeated at Woodside if management issues were not addressed quickly. Unfortunately, up to now, Bill's suggestions to George had fallen on deaf ears. George ran his business as if he expected to live forever. George was so smart in certain areas it was scary. However George seemed to think his intelligence applied uniformly across the board. Bad news. It didn't.

As soon as Bill arrived at Woodside he started putting a budget together. The financial reports were adequate, but the company had not yet initiated a budgeting process. He even got pretty good acceptance from all the department heads. Everyone except George, who just wasn't ready to apply the discipline of executing a plan involving following and managing a budget. This scenario is not atypical of entrepreneurs. Thus Bill hoped that he would be able to show George the value of this management tool.

It wasn't that George didn't exercise fiscal discipline. Such a discipline just had not become part of the "corporate fabric." The budget probably existed in some vague form in George's mind, but the whole management group needed to be involved in that discipline as well as hitting their numbers. Because the management staff hadn't been expected to do so, the focus on financial accomplishment became vague and diffused.

Not having a financial plan is like flying to a specific destination without a flight plan. You might get to your destination, but it is very unlikely without a flight plan. Why do that?

In business, common sense isn't that common. Doing the smart things in business does not always come naturally. And that's the value of a team. Ultimately a business becomes too complex for one individual to bring all the "mission critical" knowledge to the party. This is a major tripping point for a lot of entrepreneurs. Bill was optimistic that he could help George make this hurdle.

Around noon on Friday, George and Carol arrived at one of their favorite retreats in Mission Bay. They enjoyed walking the beach and just enjoying the fresh air and sand between their toes. George had always found this experience to be "head-clearing." Already the drive along the sunny shoreline had changed their mental state. The drive to the Bay had given them time to decompress, though there was little conversation. They both stuck to their thoughts. It was almost like they were laying the groundwork for deep conversations.

It was always restorative to walk the beach together and split a bottle of good wine while listening to some of their favorite soft jazz CD's. This was just right for some relaxed reflection. And the bottle of Silver Oak wasn't too bad either.

George: "I guess I missed some of the signals. Maybe it's more honest to say that I pretended not to see the signals. I'd expected that we'd receive a decent offer from Dillingham. Getting a nice payday and securing a nice retirement finally looked within reach. We have worked incredibly hard these past thirty years..." His voice trailed off.

Carol: "No George, it's thirty-five years last month!"

George winced with pain: "The last five years have seemed like 25! And we have worked too hard not to realize the value of our business. And the best exit, I think, is to sell the business. I thought we were there."

Carol: "What does Bill think? Have you discussed this with him? He has been urging us to make changes– develop a management team, develop a budget, up-grade our systems. He's been on that theme ever since he arrived. It sounds like some of the things Bill has been urging us to do fall in line with what Dillingham was concerned about. Am I right?"

George: "You know, you're right. I have been so caught up in keeping everything looking good and moving ahead while we have been in conversations with Dill-ingham that I have kind of pushed Bill's stuff off into the background."

George drew a deep breath and walked over to the window, studying the small sailboats as they came around a marker. George stood there qui-etly. He was about to slip into a reverie of sailing days gone by. Carol didn't want to disturb George. She sat quietly watching the sail boats as George was deep in thought. Slowly George turned, faced Carol, and said: "I think I'm beginning to get it."

"You know dear, I have to admit I have been reluctant to make a lot of changes. I like our management structure just the way it is. I enjoy making decisions. I enjoy being the general and making key field decisions in the heat of battle. It makes me feel like I'm accomplishing something really important. I get a lot of gratification out of running my business the way I like to run it. There, I've said it. I guess I haven't actually put it into words before. That is how I feel. Does that make sense?"

Carol: "Yes, that's how you like to run your business. However, it's killing both you and the company. Your son has certainly picked up on it. Steve was in my office a couple of days ago and we got into a conversation about the Dillingham transaction. It was looking more like a possibility a few days ago. Anyway, Steve's comment was that he didn't think you would really want to step back, much less get out of the business. He thinks this business is who you have become. It's you. You get too much of your self-worth out of what you are doing in your business. I guess I don't disagree with him. Your presence in the business is very significant. You cast a long shadow.

"Steve mentioned something else we need to discuss. Did you know he really doesn't want us to sell the business? He has fond dreams of someday running the family business for us. Have you had any recent discussions with him about his future role in the business?"

George: "No. Steve and I don't see eye to eye on several fronts. I sometimes sense that he feels a certain entitlement. He thinks he ought to end up running this business because he's our son, and not because he has the ability to do it. Sure, he is smart. He understands the industry, but I have no idea how well he would do running the business. But that is another conversation–one I don't feel like drilling into right now. We came here this weekend to make sense of where we are with our business. I just wish we had a better idea of what our options are. All I see are issues."

TRIPPING POINTS OBSERVED IN SCENE 6

1. MANAGERS NOT KNOWING THEIR NUMBERS

2. LACK OF BUDGETING

3. NO LEADING INDICATORS

4. LACK OF FISCAL DISCIPLINE

5. LACK OF COMMUNICATION OF FISCAL PERFORMANCE

COMMENTARY

FINANCIAL MANAGEMENT – BASIC TO SUCCESS

Many businesses like George's create solid success without a formal budget process, at least up to a point. Ultimately, not having a budget or a financial plan robs a business of the kind of discipline budgeting provides: spending resources on the right priorities and tracking performance against a plan. Entrepreneurs usually have an informal form of budgeting buried away in the recesses of their minds though it may not be institutionalized. In such a scenario a budget is not part of the management culture. Businesses outgrow this approach and become vulnerable.

Realizing a business owner's goals and objectives depends on financial performance. Targeting and executing the right outcomes are essential in realizing positive financial results, corporately and personally. Peter Drucker was absolutely right when he said: "Unless a business happens to be in a market with little competition, excellence is required to maintain successful operations."

A major dilemma is surfacing in emerging small-to-medium-sized businesses:

1. Entrepreneurs and managers are not keeping up with financial management processes and disciplined performance, which are required to deliver sustained success.

2. The marketplace is becoming more and more unforgiving.

FINANCIAL MANAGEMENT – SLOW TO CHANGE

Unfortunately, in too many small-to-medium sized businesses, financial management has not come of age. Managers are still making too many financial and business decisions based on "looking in the rear-view mirror" rather than taking advantage of financial analysis supported by strategic thinking. Many good financial tools are available that can help a business achieve, or surpass, its financial goals.

Just as unconscious incompetence (simply not knowing what one does not know but should know) has impacted general management, the same is true of financial management. A lot of good and valuable financial management knowledge lies dormant outside the doors of needy businesses. The essence of management is *predictability*. The better the management processes, the more predictable the results. The same is true of financial management. A strategically focused financial management process supports achieving preferred results.

In this context, we mean a strategically focused process, that has been scrubbed, tweaked and modified to *focus financial performance on the activities that will produce the results targeted in the business' strategic plan.* Budget and financial reporting must be in sync with the strategic plan. If this is not the case in your business, you may be making significant expenditures for the wrong goods and services as well as missing real profit opportunities.

A STRATEGICALLY FOCUSED FINANCIAL MANAGEMENT PROCESS SUPPORTS ACHIEVING THE RESULTS SOUGHT.

BEST PRACTICES

A careful study of the most successfully managed companies reveals common financial management practices. Almost without exception they:

- Create a sense of mission by clarifying what each work group is working toward.

- Make it easy, and a part of the culture, for everyone to know their numbers. This involves taking the complexity out of knowing where the company and each "profit center" stand in their financial performance.

- Develop a clear communication process, so the work of individuals as well as the work of the team as a whole can be clearly understood and accomplished in a timely manner.

- Identify critical financial success factors, along with the appropriate mechanism to ensure the pursuit of excellence. Then, deliver on schedule.

- Ensure there is an on-going improvement mentality, particularly aimed at cost improvement, systems improvement and the training of people operating those systems.

WHAT ELSE CAN WE DO?

Above are the functions the management team must understand and support if they are to be effective in producing superior financial performance. And this is what separates the winners from the losers. The winners continue to look for the next thing they can improve to create predictable positive financial results. Have you prepared your list of "improvement must-dos" yet?

THE BETTER THE PROCESS, THE GREATER THE PREDICTABILITY.

THE BETTER THE PROCESS, THE BETTER THE RESULTS

Each business has some form of a financial management process. These vary according to industry, size of business, sophistication of technology, as well as evolution of the business, management, and its leadership. The better the process, the greater the likelihood of achieving the desired end-point.

Take a look at your financial management. Is it delivering the kind of results that gives you comfort for the future? Just maybe there are additional things you can do to ratchet-up the predictability for positive future results. It's worthy of a hard look.

THE FINANCIAL PERFORMANCE CHECK-UP

- Do managers know their budget numbers?

- Are managers held accountable for their budget numbers?

- Do key performance indicators guide management's emphasis?

- Is the budget process integrated with the strategic plan?

- Do your stakeholders support your financial plan?

YOUR TRANSITION JOURNAL

What are some of the financial issues that come to mind that you could be addressing?

_____

_____

_____

_____

_____

_____

_____

_____

_____

IT'S NEVER TOO EARLY TO START PLANNING FOR THE FUTURE.

PERSONAL FINANCIAL OUTCOME

- KNOW WHY YOU ARE WORKING
- BALANCE RESOURCES BETWEEN BUSINESS & PERSONAL NEEDS
- THERE IS AN END POINT . . . WHAT IS IT?
- MAKING A PLAN THAT WORKS. . .AND WORK THE PLAN
- ACHIEVE PEACE OF MIND AND FREEDOM OF ACTION

"Procrastination is opportunity's assassin."

- Victor Kiam

THE TRANSITION CHRONICLES, SCENE 7

It's Sunday evening. George and Carol returned home from their trip feeling tremendously frustrated. Over the years they'd developed a caring, stable relationship. They endured their rough moments, particularly when George faced several growth crises at Woodside, and found himself overwhelmed by the choices he had to make. Carol has developed the ability to effectively read him and adjust to his moods through these stressful situations.

But the business was exacting a toll on their emotions at the moment, and that complicated everything. Both

George and Carol were quite stressed. After all, admitting that he didn't know what to do about his business was new territory for George. He had great confidence in his ability, but worried now that the business would not survive without him . . . or with him. What to do with their business right now was the burning question in his mind.

It almost seemed like this whole mess just sneaked up on them. One day they were running their business quite comfortably, making a good living, and all of a sudden it skyrocketed. Then, in the blink of an eye, they are in their 60's, wondering how they are going to retire, or at least get enough money out of their business to have some decent options.

No doubt about it—their financial "eggs" were all in the company basket. They had some money set aside in a couple of property investments that had done fine. But that would not take care of their retirement. Then there was the Steve matter. Sure, it would be nice someday to have him running the business, but was that even an option? And how could he possibly buy the business from them? It was clear that they had to get their money out of the business to retire with anything close to the lifestyle to which they'd grown accustomed.

George's stress was amplified by the fact that he couldn't remember a time he'd been faced with so many questions with answers just out of reach. He knew Bill had touched on these topics several times over the past few months, but George had been caught up in the Dillingham deal and probably wasn't listening.

That was it. He knew he needed to bring Bill into the picture and get his take on all of this. Bill seemed to be pretty level-headed. Somewhere in his career he seemed to have seen something similar to this situation. They would get together first thing tomorrow morning.

Monday morning George arrived at the office with his usual steaming Venti-sized Latte in hand. As he walked by Bill's office he noticed he was already at his PC. He poked his head in and said, "Hey Bill, good morning. Have a good weekend?"

Bill: "Sure did. Spent most of it taking the kids to their sports events. Most of Saturday was spent at a soccer tournament. How was Mission Bay?"

George: "It's hard not to enjoy Mission Bay. It's one of our favorite places. I think we had the time we needed to at least get our heads around some of the questions we are facing. When you have a minute, could you come down to my office? I would like to pick your brain on several aspects of the process we went through with Dillingham."

Bill: "Sure thing. I'll be there just as soon as I finish this email and grab a cup of coffee."

George scooted into his office, nearly tripping over his rusty putter and putting green in the corner by the windows, and slid into the desk, setting his briefcase and coffee down. Flipping on his PC, he began to peruse his email inbox. There, among the 48 emails competing for his attention, he found one from his son, Steve:. Subject: The Business. "Hey Dad, when your schedule permits, I would like to have some one-on-

one time with you to talk about the future of the business. Please let me know when you have an hour or so available that we can talk. Thanks. Steve."

George knew where that was headed. He also knew he wasn't prepared for that conversation just yet. He had too many questions on his mind to start addressing Steve's concerns. "Steve, based on several issues I'm trying to resolve around the Dillingham matter, I would like to hold off until Wednesday, okay? Sometime around 4:00 would probably work best." George had just hit "send" when Bill walked in.

Bill: "What's up?"

George: "I seem to have reached a point where the questions I have about the business far surpass any answers. Frankly, I'm a bit frustrated. The answer we got from Dillingham has really thrown me off balance. But first Bill, let me just say I realize I have been playing my cards pretty close to the vest, and we haven't really discussed some of the issues related to the next step with the business. I guess I have wanted to give you sufficient time to get your *feet under the desk*. How long have you been with us now, a year?"

Bill: "Actually, it's two years last month."

George: "I can hardly believe how fast the time has passed. Well, Bill, you seem to be taking it all in very well. I have assumed you would let me know if things were not progressing to your satisfaction. Right?"

Bill: "That's right. But now that we are on the subject, I would like to cover a couple of points, okay?"

George: "Sure. What's on your mind?"

Bill: "Well George, you seem to be performing like many entrepreneurs I have met and read about. You are running this business like you probably did when it was half this size. By not using your organization, you have created an incredibly monstrous job for yourself.

"Perhaps I should have spoken sooner; it's been on my mind for some time. I would like to be more helpful to you. I believe there are things you can off-load to make your job more manageable as well as more enjoyable. I am being under utilized, and I think some of our other managers are as well."

Looking a bit surprised, George paused, then in a raised voice began speaking: "Have you been talking to someone in the Dillingham Group? That essentially was the message they delivered to me too.

Bill: "Hold on George. I spoke with the Dillingham folks only about the financials, and then I only answered the questions they asked me. We had no conversations about you or any other managers."

George: "Okay, okay...I'm sorry. It's just that they alluded to some of the same issues. I know I get a bit over-bearing, but I usually get the results I want that way. And it just takes too much time to explain to someone else what I want. It's usually faster and better if I do it myself."

George looked out the window at the trees and lake quietly for a moment, then gazed directly into Bill's eyes and stated: "I have been running this business now for 30 years, and have done pretty well if I do say so. So what exactly are you saying?"

Bill: "Please do not take me wrong, George. You have done a terrific job of building this business. It's a great business. But it's hamstrung—it can't function very well without your direct involvement. You run the show. That is very typical of entrepreneurs, essential in the early stages of a business. But at some point, the business will become too big for one person to run the way you do. That's when businesses usually change to a team-style of management with a team of managers working together to oversee a much larger business.

"A team can achieve greater efficiency quicker than a single entrepreneur can. That is, for a business our size. No single person can cover all the bases; there are just too many decisions. Besides, the business becomes too vulnerable by becoming reliant on a single individual. In that scenario, the entrepreneur *is* the business. He's indispensable. The business just doesn't work unless he's in the driver's seat. That's pretty risky."

George became very quiet, stood up and leaned against the window, and stared out at the view for a few moments. Then, he sighed almost with relief and admitted, "Bill, you are sure saying a lot of the same things Dillingham said! Are you telling me...?"

Bill: "George, all I'm telling you is what you could read in the top five management books offered on Amazon. What I have just said is common management knowledge. I must have read this stuff for at least three or four of my MBA courses.

"But it's not just being able to spot this situation. The difficulty is responding to it. Many businesses don't, and they never reach their potential. Many business owners never realize the true value of all they have worked so hard to create. I guess in many respects the business outgrows the entrepreneur's skill sets. Their technical knowledge becomes comparatively less important. It takes well developed leadership and management skills to take an organization to its full potential. That's why many entrepreneurs bring in professional management at some point to take their business to the next level."

George: "Well, you certainly have given me a lot to think about."

TRIPPING POINTS OBSERVED IN SCENE 7

1. LACK OF GALVANIZING PURPOSE
2. PERSONAL NEEDS OVER-RIDE BUSINESS NEEDS
3. NO PLANNED EXIT
4. NO PLAN AT ALL
5. TURMOIL AND ANXIETY

COMMENTARY

KNOW WHY YOU ARE WORKING

George typifies many "old school" entrepreneurs; running his business like he expects to live forever, with few or no plans for retirement. Almost all of his financial resources are in his business. He still depends on what his business provides to meet his standard of living. The issue here is: his personal financial situation is unresolved. There is no definitive plan.

It is extremely disappointing to see a business owner reach the point in his career where he wants to enjoy the fruits of his labor–but his "fruit orchard" has not produced the results he was counting on. Unfortunately, this situation occurs far too often. It need not be so. A well executed Business Transition Plan, could change that. At least it could if launched soon enough.

A successful Business Transition Plan cannot be designed without knowing why the owner is working so hard. Meeting the future financial and emotional needs of the business owner is critical to the process. Developing the picture of the end-game–"Why are we doing this?"–provides the clarity needed to create the transition plan. "Begin with the end in mind" is highly applicable advice in transition planning.

Business owners can select from numerous options to realize the benefits of their business—provided they start in time. We cannot stress enough how important sufficient planning and execution is if you're to maximize the value of your business for yourself and all stakeholders, including loyal employees and partners.

A clear and strategic transition plan identifies all necessary milestones, and increases a business owner's probability of achieving his goals. However, this situation is far too rare. Most owners keep running their businesses as if they are immortal. Then their heirs get stuck cleaning up the estate. A huge opportunity is missed!

Another opportunity to build your business strength is to address the financial incentives of your key employees. As businesses grow and mature the focus shifts from the founder-entrepreneur contribution to the executive team's contribution. You can run faster alone, but you can run further with others. A business grows faster and stronger with a good team. Putting that team together is one of the entrepreneur's biggest opportunities.

Taking care financially of key employees is critical. You will keep the really good ones, and get great value, by making sure they are properly rewarded for their long-term contribution and loyalty. Several effective ways exist to do it without creating minority stockholders; something we advise against. The important thing is to do it. Again, take care of the people who got you where you wanted to be.

BALANCE RESOURCES BETWEEN BUSINESS AND PERSONAL NEEDS

When it comes to balancing business and personal resources, we've observed two different types of business owners. Too few create a contingency fund in their business to handle the unexpected. The majority allow their personal lifestyles to drain their business reserves. Given these two options, we recommend you balance your risks and rewards and maintain sufficient personal liquidity.

A final point here: it's both unwise and unsafe to have all of your wealth tied up in your business. Again, it's balance. Our advice: Be prepared.

THERE IS AN END POINT…WHAT IS IT?

It's never too early to start planning for the future. Ideally, start 5 to 10 years out from the desired end-point. Inventory where you are now and the resources you currently have to work with. Then create the picture of the end-point you wish to achieve. Here are three strategies to consider in realizing your goals:

1. **OPTIMIZE THE PERFORMANCE OF YOUR BUSINESS**—get it in shape to predictably deliver end-point results. If you are not sure how to get this done, get help.

2. **CREATE YOUR TEAM OF PROFESSIONALS**—these advisors will provide you the counsel and expert advice needed to enable your plan. This usually would include your attorney, accountant, and planning facilitator (such as professional financial planner). Regular progress review meetings (twice a year) will be beneficial.

3. **EXECUTE YOUR PLANS WITH GREAT DISCIPLINE**—Stay the course; make adjustments as needed. A good plan needs tending. You won't optimize your opportunity without working it.

MAKE A PLAN THAT WORKS…AND WORK THE PLAN

A lot of transition plans are never realized because of poor execution. Granted, many points of opportunity and risk exist. However, the better the execution, the higher the predictability for successful outcomes.

The problem with many execution strategies is that they are based on methods and thinking that worked in the good old days (three years ago), and no longer work today. Prominent Sci-Fi author Don Ward observed, "Remember that yesterday's answer may have nothing to do with today's problem." How do you do this? First, shift from meaningless activity to meaningful action by focusing on making decisions that move the plan forward. We must shift from improving processes to improving execution.

Perhaps it's time to stop hiding from the fact that your business has been ineffective. You can continue to fake it, or you can fix it. Your end-point (e.g. perpetuation of the business, sale of business, retirement, more leisurely life-style) can be achieved only if you execute well. Make your plan and doggedly manage it. Then, you can start looking at the travel brochures.

ACHIEVE PEACE OF MIND AND FREEDOM OF ACTION

Knowing you have your business and personal finances addressed is just good sense. Peace of mind is a desirable thing—not only for you but for your spouse/significant other and family members. A companion to peace of mind is freedom of action—you get to do what you want to do! Many good professional advisors can help you develop a plan to get to the place you want to be. Go ahead; you have earned it. Plan for the best outcome and go for it.

The Personal Financial Outcome Check-up

- Do you have an income continuity plan?

- Do you have sufficient assets outside the business to ensure a comfortable retirement?

- Is your personal debt in balance with your overall asset management?

- Do you have personal guarantees that could jeopardize personal assets?

- Could you pass the baton if it was deemed advisable?

YOUR TRANSITION JOURNAL

What are some of the personal financial issues that come to mind that you could be addressing?

_____

_____

_____

_____

_____

_____

_____

_____

_____

_____

IT IS REALLY NEW OPPORTUNITIES THAT PAVE THE WAY
TO A BETTER FUTURE

A SYSTEM TO EFFECTIVELY MANAGE CHANGE

- RESPONDING TO CHANGE
- OPPORTUNITY SPOTTING
- OPPORTUNITY SEIZING
- METHODOLOGY
- CONCLUSION

"It is not the strongest of the species that survives, nor the most intelligent that survives. It is the one that is the most adaptable to change."

- Charles Darwin

THE TRANSITION CHRONICLES, SCENE 8

Over the next few days, George and Bill had many more discussions. George also included Carol in these sessions, and she suggested a third party be brought in to provide some objectivity, as well as perspective. They just kept circling back to the same questions, for which they could develop neither reasonable nor acceptable answers. They concluded they needed outside help. Bill was reluctant to try to become George and Carol's advisor in areas he just did not have the depth of knowledge nor experience to share.

Bill was aware of a professional consulting firm that provided business transition planning services. His last firm had engaged them to facilitate their strategic planning and implementation process. They had worked together for a few months prior to Bill leaving to join Woodside. The firm had great credentials and was beginning to assist his old firm in taking actions long overdue.

At George's request Bill gave them a call and invited them in to make an assessment. George, Carol and Bill liked what they heard and the firm was engaged to assist George and Carol in developing a Business Transition Plan that would help them create some options.

After several weeks, George and Carol, with the Business Transition Specialist's assistance, were able to talk openly and discuss the Seven Critical Issues.

1. LEADERSHIP

George is a classic entrepreneur. It is quite feasible and comfortable for him to make most of the decisions, think of the next best idea, and make sure it gets implemented. Most of his direct reports simply follow orders, but should not be considered as managers. Yes, they perform the tasks the entrepreneur assigns, but seldom are called upon to be the generator of the next best ideas for taking the business forward. George developed an environment where he is the prime decision maker. Without George, there is no momentum. Everyone is waiting for their orders from George.

This is one of the key issues Dillingham spotted. No management depth or breadth. It is a "job" for George, not a free-standing business. George's perception of what he does is his job. Building a business simply has not occurred to him. As long as he is making money, in his mind he is doing the right things. He has no understanding of the life-cycles businesses go through and how the demands placed on management change at each stage.

It was observed that Woodside would benefit greatly from developing a management team: a cadre of professionals who could take the business to the next level, with or without George. Then George would have something of real value that a prospective buyer may be willing to pay for. Or, George may have a business that could be perpetuated; one that his son could run some day if properly prepared.

2. Relationships

George has difficulty finding and trusting the right people. Learning how to bring strong managers together and get them functioning as a team isn't his skill set. In addition, his managers do not know the specific steps involved in (a) committing to be a team, (b) developing the knowledge of what teamwork really is (not what many untrained business people think it is), and (c) developing the skills to make teaming really work (See Chapter 2).

Specifically, George's relationship skills are keeping him from (a) discovering all that his management team could do for the business, (b) getting his son, Steve, on a good path for increased future responsibility, and, (c) allowing his wife, Carol, to be involved openly with her staff. And this is just one facet of all the relationship issues.

3. OWNERSHIP & LEADERSHIP SUCCESSION

George's business has out-grown his ability to create the momentum requisite to sustain growth and profitability. His business has not only outgrown him, but also most likely most of his managers, as well as his systems. Very little has changed in his business model since its revenue was at $25 million. Now with Woodside generating over $70 million and being on pace to hit $85 million this year, George finally admitted he simply doesn't have the knowledge or skills to get the company there.

Dillingham's people saw Woodside's potential. But they also know it takes management to realize that potential. And it does take more work to bring a business into the current business environment that has been compromised by a major lag in their management abilities. This is not a rapid process. Every business is perfectly aligned to produce the results it's already getting. Re-alignment takes time; much baggage must be eliminated, as well as dealing with the existing staff who are essentially "order-takers." That is not meant to be unkind. But the reality is many strong entrepreneurs ultimately develop a cadre of direct reports who are waiting for their next instructions. Based on the conditioning of their culture, these employees are not opportunity-seekers. That's their boss's job. And their condition (non-opportunity seeking) usually runs deep and is not easy to change. However, the situation can be changed. These employ-

IF YOU PUT A GOOD PERSON IN A BAD SYSTEM, THE SYSTEM WILL WIN JUST ABOUT EVERY TIME.

ees may have been originally hired because they could lead change. But if you put a good person in a bad system, the system will win just about every time.

The time to start preparing for the future was last year. But getting going now is better than never starting at all. Business leadership needs to be thinking 2-3 years into the future about the organization and systems they'll need to effectively handle their business when it's 25-50% bigger–or smaller. Leadership needs to be working *on* the business as well as *in* the business. If these things are accomplished you can and will be developing options regarding your ownership as well as your leadership succession. You will also favorably impact the value of your business.

4. Strategic Planning and Implementation

The big guys usually plan pretty well. They have to or they wouldn't become or stay big guys. While planning doesn't guarantee sustained success, not doing planning is snubbing one of the oldest and best practices of human civilization. How did the pyramids get built? The Roman aqueducts? A man on the moon? These successes are a result of a combination of strategic planning and very, very good implementation.

Yes, execution is the hard part. The overwhelming tendency is to develop a plan that either gets partially implemented or not at all. This is most prevalent in the small businesses being run by technicians rather than professional managers.

OVERALL, A STRONG LEADERSHIP TEAM WILL BEAT A SINGLE LEADER ALMOST EVERY TIME.

Even professional managers often fail to get it right. Why? Because in our human nature we struggle to do all the things we know are good for us, but we lack the discipline to follow through. Much resolve is required that will either come from a very strong leader or a strong leadership team. Overall, a strong leadership team will beat a single leader almost every time in maintaining a disciplined planning and implementation process.

Woodside isn't there yet. The senior managers have no vision of the future. They have no idea what they are working for, except to please George.

5. Management Performance – Predictability & Balance

Woodside has achieved a level of success doing what they know how to do. And, rather than good business practices that are imbedded in the business, it's the sheer force of the entrepreneur's personality that drives performance. However, this process is not institutionalized. If George leaves, so does the driving force that substitutes for strong team management.

THE ECONOMIC GOOD TIMES WERE MASKING THE DANGERS OF WEAK FINANCIAL MANAGEMENT.

This was a big problem for Dillingham, though it was a blind spot for George. But he didn't possess either the knowledge or understanding of the importance of management depth and application. It's usually what you don't know that does the most damage that would make a big difference in the outcome if you were aware of it. Thus, there's the basis for the quest of knowledge and the skill to use that knowledge to create predictable success. That's what Jim Collins determined the great companies did in his best-seller, *Good to Great*.

One of the big opportunities for Woodside is introducing and implementing best business practices that would increase productivity, profitability, and predictability. Woodside is using amateur tactics in a business environment that is becoming increasingly complex and competitive.

6. Financial Performance

Like many businesses this size, Woodside has no formal budget process. They achieve a reasonable bottom line, but a lot is left on the table because the discipline of money management through a budget process is missing. On the other hand, great companies that consistently grow their profits utilize budget modeling, using leading indicators to determining what changes need to be made — before it's too late–in order to hit their budgets. Most companies fall somewhere in between.

George struggles with business discipline. The economic good times are masking the dangers of weak financial management.

Two issues surface here. First, during good times, money is being left on the table. And second, during bad times, even the table has left. There's no substitute for intelligent money management. Tough money management is often disguised as intelligent money management. Having "Dr. No" in charge of the budget often results in good opportunities missed. We need to know when to spend as well as when not to spend. Good budget administration doesn't just "happen." And it's not a book-keeper's job. It's the work of tal-

> TOUGH MONEY MANAGEMENT IS OFTEN DISGUISED AS INTELLIGENT MONEY MANAGEMENT.

ented resource strategists looking to create short and long term profitability.

Having Key Performance Indicators (KPI's) in place to highlight important performance areas is a crucial part of astute financial management. Small businesses often wrestle with a twenty page line-item budget, missing the big picture or trends that could be seen in time to take action. KPI's help make that happen.

The combination of a disciplined budget process, modeling (doing the "what ifs"), and KPI's has a significant impact on a company's ability to create predictable, successful results.

7. PERSONAL FINANCIAL OUTCOME

The Woodside picture really does represent most business owners. They hope their business is going to provide for their retirement, but they have no specific plan to make it happen with any certainty or even high predictability. No strategy is in place to increase the likelihood that they will retire in comfort, rather than leaving their heirs to restore the value of the business...if there is any value left to restore. Or, by not systematically developing personal reserves, the heirs get left with much less than they could have received.

One of the biggest problems most small business owners experience is related to lifestyle. Funding lifestyle often takes a higher priority than funding for retirement. All the family retirement "eggs" are in the business "basket." The only thing to

THE ONLY THING TO KEEP US FROM REACHING RETIREMENT AGE—WHETHER WE RETIRE OR NOT—IS DEATH. PREPARATION FOR BOTH IS SHREWD AND WISE PLANNING.

keep us from reaching retirement age—*whether we retire or not*—is death. Preparation for both is shrewd and wise planning.

Now that George was able to identify the Seven Critical Issues and acknowledged the Tripping Points, a Business Transition Plan could be designed that:

1. Identified the Tripping Points

2. Prioritized the Seven Critical Issues

3. Assigned specific responsibilities to all team members

4. Provided the management system to ensure the plan gets implemented.

THE TRANSITION CHECK-UP

- Have you identified your Tripping Points?

- Have you contacted your advisors?

- Do you know the goals & objectives of your stakeholders?

- Can you prioritize your issues?

- Do you have resolve?

Your Transition Journal

What you have just read, is fairly typical of what our firm addresses in a business engagement. We trust you will be able to identify the Tripping Points in your business that deserve thoughtful attention—now:

_____

_____

_____

_____

_____

_____

_____

_____

_____

_____

_____

COMMENTARY

RESPONDING TO CHANGE

There are many "Drucker Nuggets" that management guru Peter Drucker left us. They will continue to have significant impact on management thinking for decades to come. Here's one that really has high impact:

Great results are obtained by exploiting opportunities, not by solving problems. To produce results resources need to be allocated to opportunities rather than problems.

This nugget does not diminish the importance of solving problems. It adds the very important perspective that it is really new opportunities that pave the way to a better future. Sure, you want your operations running smoothly. But if you are not seeking the new opportunities, your organization will start falling behind in its overall competitive position in today's business environment.

And this requires a mind-set that is looking to make changes–changes that are constantly working on a platform of improvements that are in effect re-inventing the business on an ongoing basis.

OPPORTUNITY SPOTTING

As we have discussed, the key job of the executive leader is to take the company to a brighter future, while continually focusing on strengthening effectiveness and productivity. A lot of

PACE IS AN ASPECT OF LEADERSHIP THAT CONTRIBUTES TO HIGH PERFORMANCE IN A COMPETITIVE MARKET.

executives in the small and middle business sector, for whatever reasons, are losing ground in this part of their jobs. Perhaps one of the most common reasons is their jobs have changed, their businesses have grown, and new strategies and tactics are required to address the challenges of the market place.

When we get the call from a potential client, it usually has to do with a single issue pressing on the business owner. However, as our assessment deepens, multiple issues usually need attention to stabilize the business. Take a look at the checklist we designed to help our current and potential clients determine where they are in building a high performance business. You will find it in Appendix B. Maybe you can spot an opportunity for your business.

OPPORTUNITY SEIZING

In a recent meeting with both the CEO and the President of a fast growing client company, the discussion turned to their changing focus from *operational* issues to *transition* issues. This is a major, and critically important, transition. This involves the real leadership stuff–being able to identify the time to make crucial, strategic adjustment in the focus of the business. Our clients first made sure their operational processes were fine-tuned and running effectively. Once addressed, they knew they were building on a solid foundation. Then, they could focus on the opportunities that can take the business to the next level. They were prepared to identify and seize opportunities knowing their fundamental business processes were sound.

We use the term "seizing" to communicate the taking of intentional and timely action. Pace is an aspect of leadership that contributes to high performance in a competitive market. First to market, or early innovators, have a market opportunity followers don't have. Swift, but well considered, direction is an important element of the successful business profile.

TRANSITION PLANNING METHODOLOGY

We are honored to assist many businesses in their transition planning. The major purpose of this book is to call attention to what is required to successfully guide a business through the shoals of change and reach the desired end-point. So it seems appropriate to conclude with a description of our methodology–how we help our clients achieve their goals.

Essentially, there are six phases:

> **1. ASSESSMENT** – Conduct interviews and surveys to identify and understand the issues affecting the business. This includes reviewing the Seven Critical Issues identified earlier.

> **2. CREATE THE PLAN** – Identify the specific steps needed to address the issues to achieve the stakeholders' preferred results.

> **3. PRIORITIZE** – Identify the sequence of the actions to be taken so as not to interfere with the normal business demands or respond to "one's" agenda.

> **4. IMPLEMENT** – Prioritize actions needed to accomplish key goals; set due dates and accomplishment accountability.

5. Evaluate and adjust – Maintain visibility and knowledge of progress, making adjustments in response to updated information.

6. Continuous improvement – Undertake regular reviews to assure continued focus and attention on the various issues identified in the plan.

The issues addressed in the Business Transition Plan range from recruiting and hiring new executives to training existing staff; from assisting in developing budgets to coordinating personal retirement plans; from coordinating the development of buy-sell agreements to coordinating preparation of job descriptions; from training in process mapping to training in delegation. The range of projects is broad, however, all are aimed at resolving issues that challenge a potentially successful business transition. We do not hand a client a report that outlines what they should do. We assist our clients in each stage of implementation. We help our clients to get the preferred results and avoid the Tripping Points.

CONCLUSION

If you have thoughtfully considered the foregoing material, you no doubt have identified an opportunity or two. Most business leaders do. What we do know is that no organization is perfect; opportunities for improvement always exist. But, most important of all is this–your business is going to change; and to survive and be successful, you need a system to guide you through all the life cycles of a business. You can either take what you get, or get what you want. Why not get the preferred results?

We trust this information will lead you, the reader, to discover ways you can achieve better business results, better personal rewards and peace of mind.

We wish you great, successful transitions!

Kurt and Hal

Most men would rather die, than think. Many do.

- Bertrand Russell

ABOUT THE AUTHORS

KURT GLASSMAN is an executive consultant and a founding partner of LeadershipOne. Kurt specializes in business transition planning for family controlled and private companies.

Kurt is a product of a fourth generation family business. Over his 30+ year career, Kurt has started, acquired, and provided counsel to a variety of businesses and owners. He has built and led international and professional service organizations; created, through acquisition, a $50 million building materials operating entity; and developed multimillion-dollar real estate projects. More importantly, Kurt has experienced the highs and the lows of the business cycle. His first-hand experience —as a principal shareholder, CEO, investor and executive consultant—gives him a unique perspective.

Kurt began his career with an international consulting firm; was admitted to the partnership in 1986, and led the international manufacturing practice in the West Region. In 1989, he helped develop the international mergers and acquisition consulting practice on the West Coast, which led to his ultimate departure from the firm to form CGB Enterprises, a Hawaii Top 250 Company. Kurt is a graduate of the University of Southern California.

 *HAL JOHNSON* has been CEO of eight different companies in the US and the UK. His primary focus has been building management teams to produce strong performance. Earlier in his career, Hal became involved in transitioning businesses (i.e., turn-around, acquisition, merger) where he began to test some of his theories on mentoring. His system for developing managers, based on acquiring core business knowledge and building leadership and relationship skills, resulted in his first book, *Mentoring for Exceptional Performance.*

Mentoring Greatness - How to Build a Great Business, Hal's second book, is designed to help CEO's mentor through applying best business practices. As he became a business transition specialist, Hal developed a unique and effective executive development process that enables companies to help their management-leaders enhance their talents with focused business knowledge and skills.

In addition to serving on several boards of directors, Hal is Chairman and a founding partner of LeadershipOne. He consults widely and speaks regularly on how to mentor a company to greatness. He holds a Masters Degree from the University of Southern California.

APPENDIX A

Corporate Lifecycles

Effective management realizes that all organizations have a lifecycle and undergo very predictable and repetitive patterns of behavior. Each stage of development provides organizations with a unique set of challenges. How well or poorly an organization deals with these challenges has a significant impact on the success or failure of the organization.

STABLE

PRIME

ARISTOCRACY

ADOLESCENCE

RECRIMINTATION

Go-Go

BUREAUCRACY

INFANCY

COURTSHIP

DEATH

The organizational lifecycle model we embrace is adapted from the work of Dr. Ichak Adizes. The Adizes model has received broad acceptance and support by professionals in the organizational development field.

Leading an organization through the lifecycle phases is not easy, or obvious. Fundamental changes in leadership and management are required in order to have an approach that balances the amount of control and flexibility needed for each stage. Leaders who fail to understand what is needed (and not needed) can inhibit development of their companies, or plunge them into premature aging.

One key difference between the lifecycle for human being versus organizations is that living things inevitably die, while organizations need not. The "age" of a company in terms of its lifecycle is not related to its chronological age, the number of employees, or the size of its assets. Instead, the lifecycle age is defined by the interrelationship between flexibility and control. There is a fountain of youth for organizations called Prime. An organization that is in Prime has achieved a balance between control and flexibility. A Prime organization knows what it is doing, where it is going, and how it will get there. It also enjoys both high growth and high profitability. Once an organization reaches Prime, leadership must work to sustain that position.

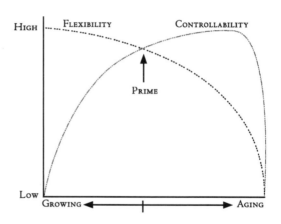

As a consulting firm specializing in business transition planning, we find the Adizes model a good convention for describing the phases of organizational development. Healthy companies are looking for ways to improve their results in the game of business. Anticipating the potential pitfalls ahead is astute management. This model enables a management team to understand the potential risks in the process of evolving and developing, and make smarter decisions. And that is precisely their job.

Business Transition Planning Survey
Assessing the Seven Critical Issues

[Please rate your current situation on each of
the following statements on a scale of 1-5]

1 = Do not agree at all
2 = Mostly do not agree
3 = Agree some of the time
4 = Mostly agree
5 = Strongly agree

#1: The Leadership Issue:

a. My colleagues would agree that I inspire all to do
   their best
b. I reward performance while I keep raising the bar
c. As a leader I create a challenging, satisfying, and
   rewarding work environment
d. Under my leadership I establish and abide by
   clear company values
e. The people in my company know where we are
   going and are very supportive

#2: The Relationship Issue:

a. Our management decision making is participative
b. Our managers cultivate relationships for
   teamwork
c. Communication in our organization is timely and
   effective
d. We have no major, or even minor, relationship
   problems
e. I can turn conflict into added value

#3: The Ownership & Leadership Succession Issue:

a. I have anticipated the need to transfer ownership at some point and have developed a plan
b. My ultimate plan provides an equitable arrangement for all of my children
c. My transition plan takes into account the perpetuation of sound management personnel
d. I have a buy/sell agreement
e. My business will be perpetuated even without me

#4: The Strategic Planning & Execution Issue:

a. We build our strategies around a clear proposition for the customer
b. We strategically keep growing our core business
c. We regularly achieve our performance targets
d. We know what we need to do in our company to consistently beat the competition.
e. We annually prepare a strategic plan and make it happen

#5: The Management Performance – Predictability & Balance Issue:

a. I have my replacement identified and in training
b. Our people are effective in meeting their work commitments
c. We have effective performance measures
d. Our management culture is results oriented
e. Our managers are effective in performance coaching

#6: The Financial Performance Issue:

a. Managers know their budget numbers
b. Managers are accountable for their budget numbers
c. Key performance indicators guide management emphasis
d. Our budget process is integrated with our strategic plan
e. I am comfortable with our banking relationship

#7: The Personal Financial Outcome Issue:

a. I have an income continuity plan
b. I have sufficient assets outside of my business to ensure a comfortable retirement
c. My personal debt is in balance with my overall asset management
d. I have no personal guarantees that could jeopardize personal assets
e. I could pass the baton if I deemed it advisable

There are a total possible 25 points in each issue category. If your category score is below 18 you have some real opportunities.

At *leadershipone.net* you can:

- Meet our people.
- Learn more about the Business Transition Planning Process.
- Explore the LeadershipOne methodology.
- Order books and articles.
- Inquire about our many programs for business improvement.
- Inquire about obtaining a speaker from our talented team.

LeadershipOne, Inc
Helping people and oganizations transition
Sacramento, CA
Email: info@leadershipone.net